No CeaseFires

No
CeaseFires

THE WAR ON POVERTY IN ROANOKE VALLEY

EDWIN L. COBB

Seven Locks Press
Cabin John, Md./Washington, D.C.

Copyright ©1984 by Total Action Against Poverty
All rights reserved

Library of Congress Cataloging in Publication Data

Cobb, Edwin L.
  No cease-fires.

  Includes index.
  1. Economic assistance, Domestic—Virginia—
Roanoke. I. Title.
HC108.R52C63 1984   362.5'58'09755791   84-5515
ISBN 0-932020-28-3
ISBN 0-932020-29-1 (pbk.)

Manufactured in the United States of America

Typography by Options Type Group, Takoma Park, Maryland
Printed by Thomson-Shore, Inc., Dexter, Michigan

Seven Locks Press

Publishers
7425 MacArthur Boulevard
P.O. Box 72
Cabin John, Maryland

Seven Locks Press is an affiliate of Calvin Kytle Associates

To W. Astor Kirk,
Regional Director for DELMARVA Region
of OEO and CSA, 1968-1981,
whose belief in and dedication
to community action
made this book possible.

FOREWORD

by Cabell Brand

PEOPLE ASK ME: Why do I, a businessman, spend so much of my time with a federally assisted community action agency?

The question, I suppose, is natural. I'm known to be deeply committed to free enterprise.* I have been an active member of the U. S. Chamber of Commerce. I am a bank director. I have participated in the Young Presidents Organization, the World Business Council, and the Chief Executives Organization. Like most of my colleagues in these organizations, I believe in the free market and am wary of excessive regulation. I would like to see a balanced federal budget and I'm interested in as little government as possible. I believe in people helping themselves.

Why then, people ask me, did I take six months off in 1965 to organize Total Action Against Poverty, the community action agency in our six-city, five-county area of the Roanoke Valley? Why have I stayed on these past twenty years as TAP's chairman? Why do I continue to advocate community action when the president of the United States, who presumably speaks for business, says community action is unnecessary if not un-American?

My answer is simple. I am convinced that the greatest danger to a free society is the perpetuation of an underclass

---

Cabell Brand is chairman and chief executive officer of The Stuart McGuire Company, Inc., a national direct-selling and mail-order operations firm.

that neither participates in, nor benefits from, that society. I believe that this underclass is the spawning bed of crime, violence, disease, class antagonism, and revolution. I believe that maintenance of this underclass makes excessive demands on the public treasury and the business economy, that it restricts our civil rights, and that it is largely responsible for the obsessive fear of crime among so many ordinary citizens in our cities and towns.

Poverty, in short, is a disease that threatens the entire body politic. If our society is to survive, poverty must be controlled if not eliminated. That's a task for all seasons. The war on poverty is not for summer soldiers.

In the twenty years that I have been with TAP, being to some degree a national spokesman for community action, I have seen gratifying progress. It is not by accident—certainly not, as some would have us believe, a result of natural, reliable, and mysterious forces of the free market—that during this time poverty in America was reduced by 40 percent. Still, I am as troubled today almost as much as I was in 1965 by the appalling misconception that most Americans have—indeed, seem to want to have—about the extent of poverty, the causes of poverty, and, perhaps most of all, the importance of federally assisted community action agencies in reducing poverty.

In 1965 twenty-one percent of the American people were in poverty, falling below the economic guidelines that at the time defined a family of four as poor if its annual income was less than $3,000. In 1980 that 21 percent had fallen to 13 percent, although the economic guidelines, adjusted for inflation, now set the poverty floor at $8,414. Unhappily, from 1979 to 1981 the number of persons in poverty began to go up again, rising to about 15 percent of the population. All told, 8.3 million Americans were added to the poverty rolls during that period—a 32 percent increase in the number of poor in four years. Today, tragically, one fifth of all U.S. children live in poverty families.

Most of this increase can be attributed to the Reagan administration's cut in social programs.

Ironically, despite the overall reduction in the *percentage* of Americans in poverty since 1964, the actual number of definable poor has again risen to a level comparable to that reflected in the 1960 census. In 1960, approximately 22.4 percent, or 39.5 million persons, were living in poverty. Now, although only 15 percent of the population, the number of poor stands at 34 million. That's substantially greater than the total population of Canada, and larger than the total population of a hundred of the world's countries.

Imagine, if you will, what the social and political pressures on our society would be had the trend since 1965 been reversed—if the percentage of our people in poverty had increased by 40 percent, instead of decreased. Based on this premise, we can estimate that had it not been for community action during this period the number of poor today would not be 34 million but 50 million.

While obviously a lot of forces combined to reduce the percentage of poor since 1965, I am convinced that the network of community action agencies, which once numbered more than a thousand, deserves much of the credit. A continuing misconception is that these agencies have been a drain on the federal budget and that they have served only to do things already being done better by traditional welfare agencies. Much of what follows in this book will, I think, prove the contrary. Let me simply emphasize here that of all domestic spending in 1983 only eight percent in cash went to aid the poor. Of that eight percent, community action agencies received no more than $330 million. We spent as much or more to refit the battleship New Jersey.

Community action agencies are public-private partnerships, locally funded, locally managed and controlled, with volunteer boards of directors. They thus constitute a type of program that President Reagan and other politicians claim to be in favor of. But politicians win few votes by championing the poor and disadvantaged. Moreover, all government is more representative of the majority than of any minority, and this is the major reason that local governments have never initiated substantive programs for the poor. Very little in my experience with TAP has persuaded me to change the opinion I expressed in a letter to President Lyndon Johnson in 1969: "The majority of the American people are not interested in the problems of the disadvantaged. They do not care. They feel that in this land of supposedly equal opportunity no one needs to be given special help by the government at taxpayers' expense."

The majority still doesn't care enough. Otherwise, why would it have allowed the Reagan administration to turn its back on the poor in favor of trickle-down economic theories that primarily benefit the well-to-do? Why would it have permitted the abolition, first of the Office of Economic Opportunity, then of the Community Services Administration? Why does it respond indifferently to the President's relentless effort to do away with all community action?

For much of the public misunderstanding, we in community action are partly to blame. Acknowledging the opposition at the local level, framers of the original law provided that community action agencies could function and be federally funded whether they had local government support or not. Here in my own Roanoke Valley, the Bedford County board of supervisors said, in 1965, that they did not want anti-poverty programs; they didn't want to participate in Head Start or in any other early childhood education programs; they saw no need for manpower training. With federal funds and the support of private citizens, we were able to start the programs anyway.

Nevertheless, because of this local hostility, we decided to take a low profile, use the available federal resources, get support from those community groups who *did* understand, and try not to arouse open opposition from our local governments. We sought very little publicity, issued few press releases, and very carefully avoided anything that might be seen as programmed public relations.

This may have been a mistake. We may have waited too long to tell our story. Over the past twenty years we have learned which anti-poverty programs are cost-effective and which are not. The time has come to capitalize on our experience, for local and state governments to institutionalize those programs that have been proven to work, so they won't be totally dependent on Washington. But for this to be done, for community action to continue, for the war on poverty to be successfully pursued and for our free economy to endure, it is necessary that the middle majority of our people come to understand the problem and support the solution.

It is my earnest hope that by describing our experience in Roanoke Valley, and by identifying the cost-effective programs amenable to national replication, *No Cease-Fires* will help achieve that understanding.

May, 1984

EDWIN L. COBB is a writer, a political scientist, and a recognized authority on problems incidental to rural water supply and waste disposal such as environmental health, housing, and economic development. To his credit are more than ten books on various aspects of both policy and technology in the rural water-sewer fields.

Since 1980 Mr. Cobb has been executive director of the National Demonstration Water Project in Washington, D.C. He holds an A.B. Degree from Delta State University in Cleveland, Mississippi, and earned both a Masters (foreign affairs) and a Ph.D. (political science) from George Washington University.

CONTENTS

Foreword by Cabell Brand   vii

Author's Preface   xv

Introduction   1

1   Waxen Poor   13

2   Warriors   28

3   Total Action Against Poverty   52

4   Making a House a Home   76

5   Going Straight   104

6   TAP Water   120

7   Toward a New Declaration   132

Epilogue   154

Index   165

AUTHOR'S PREFACE

This book argues that poverty is the dark underside of American opportunity, that the task before us is to eliminate that poverty, and that the best instrument for accomplishing the task is an adequately funded and federally supported community action program. In reaching that conclusion, the book focuses on the experience of one community action agency, Total Action Against Poverty—TAP—in Roanoke, Virginia.

This is not a complete history of TAP. A full description and analysis of all the programs the agency has operated would require many volumes. Instead, the book looks at the moods and essences of TAP and attempts to distill the experiences that seem most relevant for the future of community action. In this distillation process, many good programs have no doubt been passed over lightly or omitted altogether. But TAP's greatest long-run contribution to the fight against poverty is not contained in any single program. TAP's strength grows from a willingness to identify new victims of poverty, such as women and ex-offenders, and to work creatively with individuals and groups for real and lasting reform.

Many people gave their time in the preparation of this book and agreed to be interviewed for the record. The unedited words of many appear in these pages. Those whose names do not appear may be sure that they were heard and that their ideas are reflected in the text. The persons interviewed were Lin Atkins, Cabell Brand, Shirley Brand, Ben Bray, Betty Brown, Raleigh Campbell, Charlene Chambers, Louise Crosby, Joliet Croson, Gloria Cumby, Betty Desper, Ted Edlich, Doris Elam, George Franklin, Corinne Gott, Byron Haner, Elizabeth Hardin, Patricia Henry, Billy Hoffman, Sara Holland, S. W. Hylton, Jim Jones, Muriel Kranowski, Joseph Kyle, Betty Long, Shirley Markhoff,

Gail Mayhew, Lynn McGhee, Georgia Meadows, Julian Moore, Ivory Morton, Martha Ogden, Osborne Payne, Anne Poskocil, J. C. Reynolds, Joel Schlanger, Abdul Shakir, Cleo Simms, Elaine Stinson, Mary Terry, Anna Mae Thomas, Jayne Thomas, Jane Tower, Elizabeth Traylor, Wilma Warren, and Iretha Woodliff.

There are four people who should receive special mention because their assistance in the preparation of the manuscript was invaluable. They are Ted Edlich of TAP, who wrote the epilogue; Stephanie Faul of Lazy Brown Associates, Washington, D.C.; Mary E. Morgan of the Institute of Rural Water, Washington, D.C.; and Anne Poskocil of Total Action Against Poverty, Roanoke, Virginia.

Finally, I am extremely grateful for the patience and encouragement given to me by Cabell Brand and Ted Edlich, and for the inspiration given to me by Bristow Hardin.

Edwin L. Cobb
Washington, D.C.
December 1983

INTRODUCTION

I hate to say this, but it's been a beautiful life so far.

Bristow Hardin to Mike Ives, August 20, 1973

THE OLD FLOUR MILL looming over Shenandoah Avenue had its face lifted years ago, and the sign now proclaims it to be the headquarters of an organization called TAP—Total Action Against Poverty in the Roanoke Valley. Inside, an attractive secretary keeps watch over a modern reception room. A telephone console buzzes on the spacious desk; and designer colors brighten the nearby stairway.

But the eye of the visitor is drawn to the portrait on the wall, the shock of reddish hair and the slightly florid face. The eyes are intent, and the mouth is set as if it were about to roar, as it had roared so often, "No shoddy performances." And the visitor realizes that in order to know TAP, one must know Bristow Hardin.

His personality dominated the organization during the ten years he commanded it, and his presence still reverberates through the corridors of this building, which now bears his name. Had Bristow lived, TAP may never have known whether it was winning the war against poverty because community action was the best way to fight such a war or because, as someone said, "we had this character down here."

More than any other single event, the death of Bristow forced TAP to examine where it had been and where it

1

wished to go, forced it to weather the type of transition that is the ultimate test of organizational strength, forced it to reaffirm its faith, renew its hope, and rekindle its charity. And so, when I think of that portrait, I think of the story of TAP—of people and poverty and community action—and of the generous and generating spirit of Bristow Hardin.

'An Influence Broad and Deep'

PRIMITIVE PEOPLE thought that the summer solstice was a sign of God's anger because he stopped the sun and made it go in the other direction. Well, God did not seem to be angry this June 21 in the year of Our Lord one thousand, nine hundred, and seventy-five. The sky was blue and clear at noon, and the sun was warm and friendly at Smith Mountain Lake.

Bristow Hardin, Jr., sat in the driver's seat of his orange Volkswagen bus as he waited for Stephen to bring the boat around from the cabin to the marina for gas. There were plenty of boats already out on the lake, and Bristow wanted to be there too. Born in Tidewater, Virginia, and a former Navy enlisted man, he could never stay away from water long. He had come to the Roanoke Valley partly because his wife, Teeny, was a Front Royal girl and loved the mountains, but he knew he would go back to the sea someday. Bristow grimaced as he thought of the times he had driven from Roanoke to Virginia Beach at breakneck speed so he could splash in the surf churned up by an approaching hurricane.

Saunders' Marina, where the Volkswagen bus sat, was a combination marina and country store. Boat people gathered there winter and summer to buy groceries, swap stories, and launch their boats. Some of them were members of the Virginia Inland Sailing Association. A friend had once

2

proposed Bristow for membership ("I didn't want to join the damn thing, anyhow"), but Bristow was known as a maverick who sometimes had guests who were, to much of Virginia society, the wrong color; so Bristow was blackballed. Whereupon he painted a large black ball on a white flag and proudly sailed around the lake.

Bristow glanced at the water again, but Stephen had not yet arrived. He shifted in his seat and waited. He was a big man, under six feet tall but thick in the chest, with reddish hair and beard. He hated to be told he looked like Burl Ives, but he did, and people told him anyway. He felt a twinge in his chest.

Bristow had been having pains for the last two weeks, but he had an EKG the previous Monday and it looked okay. He used to tell Teeny that he doubted he would make it to 40, and here he was 52. Teeny never nagged about his heavy smoking and overeating. "I like to eat," he once screamed at her. What with camping and boating, he did get lots of exercise. Besides, his father had had heart trouble all his life and was still going strong as he approached 80.

His father. Bristow had recently made up with his dad after a long estrangement caused by their different racial views. But Bristow doubted his father would ever really get over the fact that Bristow's daughter had married a black man. His father loved to play with his great-granddaughter, Amber, but deep down he could never accept interracial marriage or even social integration for that matter.

With the noonday sun beating down, it was hot inside the bus, and Bristow wiped the sweat from his face and neck. He perspired more than most people, and his socks and underwear always seemed to be wet in summer. Once when he and Teeny were moving, he had griped and groused about "all the crap" they had to move. Teeny was tired and finally got exasperated. She had burst out at him, "If you didn't have to have 50 changes of underwear and socks, we wouldn't have so much crap."

3

When Bristow saw Stephen approaching with the boat, he got out of his bus and started toward the landing. He was dressed in his usual get-up—khaki shorts that were too big for him (the result of a crash diet), leather moccasins with no socks, and a blue Caribbean-style shirt. The shirt was one from the line that Cabell Brand had bought in Puerto Rico. Cabell's family owned a clothing company in Salem, which adjoined Roanoke, and Cabell had been the chairman of Bristow's board of directors since TAP began.

The thought of Cabell always made Bristow smile. They disagreed sometimes, and Cabell never cared for Bristow's foul language, but how could you get mad at Cabell, a patrician Virginia businessman who had spent ten hard years busting his ass for a shirttail community action agency that tried to help poor people? Total Action Against Poverty in the Roanoke Valley—TAP—they had christened it in 1965, and although Bristow, Cabell, and others had had to fight many a battle, they had won just about all of them. Plans were in the works for TAP's tenth anniversary celebration.

In spite of the headaches, Bristow loved his job, loved "making the big decisions," as he frequently said. But, God, the problems poor people had in the Roanoke Valley! They lived in shacks with no running water; they got poor schooling and couldn't get jobs; they sometimes had to go without food or heat; their kids were on drugs or in jail. A warm sunny day like this Saturday in June was almost, but not quite, enough to make a person forget all that.

Stephen and the boat were at the landing now. Stephen was the youngest of Wilma Warren's four children. She and Bristow had been friends and co-workers for many years and he was now, as executive director, her boss at TAP. She and the Hardins had bought the cabin at the lake in 1970, and one or both families used it practically every weekend in the summer. This afternoon they were holding a birthday party for George Grote, who ran Hegira House, a halfway house for drug addicts in Roanoke.

4

"Stephen, I think you'll have to lift those cans up to me," said Bristow as he clambered onto the boat, "I've been having some pains lately." The fourteen-year-old Stephen handed up the heavy cans, and Bristow began to fill the tank with gasoline. The last can was too full, and as he started to pour, gasoline splashed down on Bristow's leg. "God damn it!" he began, and once started, there was no stopping him. He filled the air with a barrage of four-letter words directed at no one in particular.

People near the landing froze at Bristow's blasphemous outburst. But Stephen, who knew Bristow and his harmless blow-ups, began to laugh. And soon the others joined in. Before long, Bristow himself was roaring with laughter.

The laughter reminded Bristow of the time when he and Teeny lived in Charlotte, North Carolina, where he was teaching high school. Teachers made very little money, and with children, it was damned hard to make ends meet. Every penny counted. They had stopped at a variety store, and Teeny had sent him to get some essential item; he could no longer remember what. Inside, he saw the most beautiful bicycle pump he had ever seen. Bristow had a broken-down bicycle but had not ridden it for years. Nevertheless, he had to have that pump. When he came out of the store proudly brandishing his new, expensive bicycle pump, Teeny at first looked like she wanted to cry, but then she started laughing, and she laughed and laughed.

The gassing-up complete, Bristow told Stephen to wait a minute, that he had to get some brochures about Boston whalers from the store. Bristow loved those sailing boats; he owned one and sold several others. Inside the marina, Bristow asked about the brochures, and the woman on duty led him to the office in the rear of the store. As she turned her head to get what Bristow had asked for, she heard a loud noise and whirled around to see him lying on the floor in the doorway. He had had a heart attack.

The Hardin-Warren cabin was located on the second road up from the marina going toward the point. The sign said "Slyvan Drive," but it was really "Sylvan Drive"; the old sign had been replaced and the new sign painter was not a good speller.

Waiting at the cabin, Wilma and Teeny wondered why Bristow was not back yet. He had cooked a pancake breakfast for them that morning, and the three of them had sat talking for a long while, the women complaining because the party for George had been arranged through Bristow, who had not bothered to consult them.

Wilma was standing near the stove when she saw Teeny leave the porch. A man, wearing a white shirt and pants, had driven up to the back of the house. Wilma ran out of the house and joined them in time to hear the man, who was a rescue worker, tell Teeny that she should come with him; he was afraid her husband had suffered a heart attack.

Mrs. Saunders from the marina had followed the rescue vehicle in her car, and Wilma rode with her. "There were two rescue people from Roanoke at the marina," said Mrs. Saunders, "and they gave him artificial respiration until the ambulance came, but they never got a pulse. I think it's too late." It was. Bristow died without regaining consciousness.

The Hardin home was in the fashionable southwest portion of Roanoke, but it was modest and modestly furnished. On Sunday, many who loved Bristow came by to pay their respects to Elizabeth Hardin, who had been called "Teeny" since childhood when her little brother could not pronounce her name.

Ted Edlich and his wife had spent the weekend at Pipestem Park. When they got home, Wilma called with the news, and they went to Bristow's house to join the others. Ted had long been a protege of Bristow and was now director of Human Services Training.

Among those at the house was the Right Reverend William H. Marmion, bishop of the Episcopalian Diocese of Southwest Virginia and a close friend of the Hardins, who were parishioners of St. John's Episcopal Church. Ten years ago, the executive committee of the diocese had passed a formal resolution supporting the antipoverty program.

Bristow had experienced a moving religious conversion as an adult. The whole thing, he decided, was forgiveness. Although he knew little about the Bible, he decided to become a priest. But he cared little for differences in creeds or interpretations of Scriptures; to him, it was enough to have faith, and he regarded the pedantic theological questions put to him by clergymen as "horse shit." The church, he decided, was just another institution, like the schools, that needed reform. Bristow worked very hard to integrate the church racially and was rewarded with hate phone calls and harassment of his children.

Bristow had a standard speech, which he gave before congregations and other audiences, regarding his views of religion. He would rise, adjust his glasses, and go on the attack. "Today, I'm going to do something that some of you might consider divinely inspired: I am going to proselytize. Today it seems fashionable not to believe in miracles. Of course, this is nonsense. As proof of a recent miracle, I submit to you, that in spite of my conversion and in spite of my recently inspired revelation, I've remained in the Episcopal Church and stand before you as an Episcopalian who is concerned with your souls. And I am here right now to offer you the same means of salvation by joining my church. It's a comparatively new denomination which offers mankind the opportunity to put into action many of the pious, holy, and humanitarian cliches we have been mouthing throughout the centuries. The name of this denomination is the *Judeo-Christian Holy Catholic Protestant Evangelical Ecumenical Reformed CAP Church.*" The Community Action Program thus became a familiar part

7

of Sunday services, and of the social doctrine, in the Roanoke Valley.

On this Sunday, Bishop Marmion's wife called Wilma Warren aside. "I really don't know how to say this, but Bill would like to be in the processional at the funeral services." Wilma spoke to Teeny, and the bishop was promptly invited. He was to join nearly a dozen other clergymen in the processional. The profane, irreverent, anti-Church Bristow had left his mark on organized religion.

The funeral would not be held until Tuesday because Jim Jones, then in Florida, could not get to Roanoke until then. Bristow and the Reverend Jones had been close friends. But then, Bristow had so many friends.

On Monday, Cabell Brand asked the entire TAP staff to attend a meeting at St. John's Church.

Cabell was tall and handsome with the bearing of a Virginia gentleman, which he was. The Brand family had been in Salem before Roanoke existed and was related to former Governor William Cabell. A frequently repeated but unverified story even traced the family back to certain illegitimate activities of Thomas Jefferson.

Today, Cabell spoke quietly of the loss they had all suffered but reminded them that Bristow had lived life to the fullest and would be disappointed if they gave in to grief too much. Bristow once said: "I keep telling people that how much money you make isn't important. It's how you live that counts." Cabell was reassuring about the future of TAP. Although Bristow's leadership had been very unorthodox and personalized, he had built, in TAP, a strong institution that could survive his passing. He had been an inspiration to them all and had set a course they could follow. The style of work that had been characteristic of TAP under Bristow would continue.

When he finished, Cabell invited others on the staff, if they chose, to talk about what Bristow had meant to them. When she rose to speak, Wilma Warren cried for the first time since the man in the white clothes had come to the back of the cabin.

After the general meeting, Cabell, Teeny, and the senior staff of TAP met at TAP headquarters to assess the situation and make plans for the future. Charlene Chambers, deputy director, was later to be made acting executive director until the TAP board could appoint a successor to Bristow. A slender, attractive black woman, Charlene had joined TAP as a Head Start teacher in the late 60s and had come up through the ranks. As quiet as Bristow was boisterous, she accepted her responsibility solemnly.

At the staff meeting, Cabell suddenly decided that Bristow's anchor should be displayed during the memorial service. Not long before, the Reverend James Stamper, former head of TAP's planning development and recently with the Virginia state government, had given Bristow a ship's anchor, and it was still in the hallway at the Hardin home. Jane Tower, who was active in St. John's Church, was dispatched to seek permission from Rector Clay Turner to display the anchor. He assented to the unusual request, and the anchor was suspended above the church altar.

St. John's Church, at the corner of Jefferson Street and Elm Avenue in southwest Roanoke, is one of the largest Episcopal churches in Virginia. It was the first to donate space for a day-care center when TAP started its program ten years earlier, and it had remained active in the poverty war. On this morning in June, the sanctuary overflowed, not only with members of the Roanoke community, but with people who had come great distances. Community action agencies in other parts of Virginia brought busloads of people.

The normal Episcopal service does not include a eulogy, but Teeny had requested one, and the rector had consented. It was given by Ted Edlich, whose long dark hair and beard gave him an appearance not unlike popular renderings of Jesus.

Ted spoke quietly. It was, he said, not a time of sadness, but a time of joy. Bristow had taught them how to work and to play, how to love each other and love life. Death was an inevitable part of life, but people should look primarily to earthly fulfillment. Bristow once told a Presbyterian group:

> The job ahead of us is enormous. Quite frankly, it sometimes is almost beyond my comprehension. But so is the thought of heaven. We Christians, while believing in heaven, must live somewhere between heaven and earth. Our visions and dreams of heaven can be used creatively to find more and more ways to bring about a better world for man.

Bristow had used his dreams creatively. According to Ted:

> Bristow's influence was broad and deep. Broad in the number of lives he touched through personal contact and in the organizations which bore his imprint. . . . So deep was his imprint that it is literally impossible to think who we would be had we not known him. One thing for sure, we would have been much poorer and Roanoke far the worse.

As friends and relatives slowly filed out of the church, the organist played "A Mighty Fortress Is Our God."

Many people felt that TAP *was* Bristow, the "mammoth stimulus on the horizon," in Ted's words, the fortress in which all took shelter. Now the fortress was no more, and TAP had to face what was likely to be its greatest challenge. The loss of a leader whose personal style plays a role in organizational affairs is a blow that few institutions can withstand. Could TAP make a leadership transition successfully? Was TAP just Bristow?

The TAP board appointed a committee—Nancy Barbour, Anna Mae Thomas, Joe Kyle, Howard Johnson, and Cabell Brand—to search for a new executive director. The job was advertised in Roanoke, Richmond, and Washington, D.C., and some thirty people applied, but it was generally assumed that the position would be filled by someone from the TAP staff. A prime qualification for the job was an understanding of how TAP worked, and no outsider could really have this expertise. Jim Stamper and Roger Ford, who was then TAP manpower director, declined to be considered for the executive director position. Fourteen TAP staffers were interviewed, but only four actually applied—Ted, Wilma, Charlene, and Bill Hoffman, a young black man who had been in TAP's training division for years. This group, with Bristow, had always been a kind of family, a TAP inner circle. To some extent, all were disciples of Bristow—Charlene possibly less than the others—and would be logical choices as his successor.

After a fifty-minute discussion, the board of directors made its selection on Tuesday, July 15. The choice was unanimous. The new executive director would be Ted Edlich; Bill Hoffman would fill Ted's spot in Human Services Training; Wilma and Charlene would remain in their same positions.

The *Roanoke Times*, while admitting that Bristow's shoes would be hard to fill, editorialized that the board had made a wise choice:

> . . . that TAP has succeeded better than many antipoverty agencies is in no small part because of the magnetism and forcefulness of Bristow Hardin. By diligence and persistence he built a bridge of trust between the establishment and the poor. Someone who worked alongside him seems best fitted to maintain that trust and, with it, TAP's momentum.

When informed by the board of his selection, Ted said that he held the job of TAP executive director in higher esteem than any other job. He added, "We're going to work hard and have a good time, like Bristow taught us." In a memorandum sent three days later to all TAP employees and "members of the TAP family," Ted gave his vision of TAP's future:

> We have all worked together with Bristow to shape the TAP community, and you can be sure that I intend to preserve the great things TAP stands for. . . .

People here at TAP will continue to be encouraged to date to do "the crazy things that sometimes work.". . . While each person will be expected to do his/her best with excellence, we are one organization and one family which works together. We are all TAP, first and foremost. I intend to work with everyone here to see that TAP not only survives, but survives gloriously.

. . . Survive gloriously. The visitor can almost hear Bristow bark this as a command, a valedictory. And TAP has survived, in many ways gloriously. It has continued its assault on the familiar causes of poverty while, at the same time, identifying and addressing new causes. Having earlier fended off the blows of Richard Nixon and his designated hitter Howard Phillips, it lived through the benign neglect of Jimmy Carter and is battling the backlash of Reaganomics.

Bristow is gone. But the poor remain. And TAP remains. And the task of maintaining the trust between the poor and society remains. And so it is that Bristow's story becomes TAP's story.

1

WAXEN POOR
A Declaration of War

The eighth and most meritorious degree of charity is to anticipate charity by preventing poverty.... To this Scripture alludes when it says: And if thy brother be waxen poor, and fallen in decay with thee, then thou shalt relieve him.

Moses Maimonides, twelfth century

AMERICA DECLARED a war on poverty in 1964, the thunderous commitment coming in the March 16 State of the Union address by President Lyndon B. Johnson: "This administration here and now declares unconditional war on poverty in America. It will not be a short or easy struggle, but we will not rest until that war is won. The richest nation on earth can afford to win it. It cannot afford to lose it."

A poverty worker in 1975 reflected on the conditions that led to this declaration:

In the early 1960s the poor were invisible and forgotten by the four-fifths of the people who had "made it" in the postwar surge to prosperity.... Every family had a mother and father who took care of each other and their clean, good children. They lived in the safe suburbs, with little to worry about except whether Wally made the football team or learned to accept "second string" with grace. Everyone was white except some big league baseball players and a few entertainers. The slums were increasingly being hidden by superhighways and concrete overpasses into our cities. The poor were a powerless minority. The welfare programs and private charities did not begin to meet their needs, and the work ethic and separate-but-equal laws had ingrained in both the middle class and the poor a surety that poor people were lazy and inferior. Only a small percentage of people believed that the 1954 Supreme Court decision would, or should, be implemented. In addition, few people had done serious thinking about poverty and its causes.

America's approach to poverty has always been ambivalent, as one would expect from a self-styled "land of opportunity." Almost every citizen has ancestors who arrived in this country possessing little more than a change of clothing and the will to work. Every immigrant came to build a better life, one that could be passed on to his children. This ideal of the self-made person is deeply ingrained in the national character; the Protestant work ethic is not limited to Protestants. According to this view, poverty is a temporary condition, and any individual can conquer it with diligence, application, and plain hard work.

The American middle class is packed with the formerly poor and their children. Millions of penniless newcomers started businesses, saved their money, moved to better neighborhoods, and brought children into a substantially better world than the one their parents had known. No one, the theory said, had to be poor. This is America, where anyone can grow up to be president.

The civil rights movement helped expose this idea as a great oversimplification. How could someone who had never been taught to read get a job? The concept of "disadvantage" became current; many Americans had always been poor, and they did not know how to be anything else.

There had been massive programs to help the poor, of course. But the programs of Roosevelt's New Deal had been aimed at those impoverished people who were willing, ready, and able to hold jobs, people for whom having no money was a relatively recent state of affairs. The unemployed, who were suffering the brunt of the Depression's disastrous economic climate, were cared for. Job creation and other incentives, such as the WPA, helped to get workers back into production. These programs had been successful; by the middle of the century, unemployment had fallen, and the average worker's standard of living had risen dramatically.

The condition of those trapped on the bottom of the economic spectrum, however, was unchanged. The civil rights movement helped to highlight the plight of those unable to participate in the postwar economic boom. The workers who had successfully mastered the American economic system began to feel guilty for not sharing their wealth; they saw that an intractable layer of poverty remained at the bottom of society. In a country that stockpiled millions of bushels of surplus wheat, people were starving.

Poverty was pushed to the forefront of the national consciousness from a number of directions. Social activists had been at work in may communities in the early 1960s, and they saw the poor firsthand. When John F. Kennedy campaigned for the presidency in 1960, he too got an on-the-ground look. While driving to victory in the pivotal West Virginia Democratic primary, he saw the bleak existence of Appalachian coal miners, and he vowed to "return to West Virginia" much as General MacArthur had vowed to return to the Philippines.

In 1962, Michael Harrington's grim portrayal of poverty, *The Other America*, was published. Harrington described in graphic detail a migrant worker, a heroin addict, and others on the fringe of society, and his message was clear: a responsible civilization could not afford to ignore so many of its citizens.

Walter Heller, who was chairman of Kennedy's Council of Economic Advisers, loaned a copy of *The Other America* to the president, who set his people to work shaping the issue of poverty as a central theme for the campaign of 1964. It was a campaign Kennedy would never fight; he was assassinated in Dallas in the fall of 1963.

When Johnson succeeded to the presidency, he had no difficulty adopting the poverty issue as his own. He thought of himself as a child of poverty and a New Deal disciple.

Eradicating poverty was "his kind of program." The war on poverty thus became an important part of the push toward the Great Society.

That the people of America "be waxen poor" was hardly a matter of dispute. In his declaration of war, Johnson ticked off some of the 1964 indicators of poverty and alluded to some of the causes:

- One-fifth of all American families and nearly one-fifth of the total population were poor.
- Of the poor, 22 percent were non-white, and nearly one-half of all non-whites lived in poverty.
- The heads of over 60 percent of all poor families had only grade school educations.
- Of all non-white families headed by a person with eight years or fewer of schooling, 57 percent were poor.
- When non-whites were compared with whites at the same level of education, non-whites were poor about twice as often.
- One-third of all poor families were headed by a person over 65, and almost one-half of all families headed by such a person were poor.
- Of the total poor, 54 percent lived in cities, 16 percent on farms, and 30 percent were non-farm rural residents.
- Over 40 percent of all farm families were poor, and more than 80 percent of all non-white farmers lived in poverty.
- Less than half the poor were in the South, but the chance of a southern resident's being poor was roughly twice that of persons living elsewhere in the country
- One quarter of all poor families were headed by a woman, but nearly one-half of all families headed by a woman were poor.
- A family headed by a young woman who was non-white and had less than an eighth-grade education was poor in 95 of 100 cases.

In sum, one-fifth of the people in the most affluent nation on earth were poor, with racial discrimination and lack of education seemingly the chief causes. And it was clear that the biggest obstacle to eliminating poverty was the tendency of the monster to reproduce itself. The poor had limited access to education, to health care, to jobs—the very things they needed to bring them from poverty. This dead-end situation bred disillusionment and killed hope. The legacy of poverty passed from parents to children. Any assault on poverty would have to address the cycle as well as the condition.

The Coming of Community Action

The Economic Opportunity Act, the legislative charter for the poverty war, was signed into law on August 20, 1964. It represented the final package emerging from a presidential task force headed by Sargent Shriver. In a way, it was radical legislation because it meant planned and massive social investments and structural changes in the system for allocating resources. But this was the concept that Harrington and others sold to Shriver and which Shriver, in turn, sold to President Johnson. Johnson badly wanted to complete the work begun under the New Deal, and he also wanted to be remembered as a president who made great improvements on the domestic front. The war on poverty was accordingly entrusted to an entirely new agency, the Office of Economic Opportunity (OEO), rather than an existing cabinet department, such as Labor or Health, Education, and Welfare. The poverty war would be commanded from the protective circle of the White House, and Shriver, who already headed a Kennedy showpiece, the Peace Corps, would, as OEO director, be the chief of staff.

The Economic Opportunity Act created a Job Corps to establish training centers where teenaged dropouts could complete their education and learn a trade. It also created Volunteers in Service to America (VISTA), a kind of

17

domestic Peace Corps, and a Neighborhood Youth Corps, which provided jobs for youths while they remained in school. Head Start education, legal aid, and neighborhood health centers were added later.

Probably the most significant title in the legislation was Title II, which introduced the concept of community action. Under this provision, local public agencies could establish community action programs (CAPs) and receive federal funding for these programs through OEO. Designated community action agencies (CAAs) could receive 90 percent federal funding to attack poverty at the community level; the remaining 10 percent had to be contributed by local agencies.

Community action programs began springing up all across the country. Although funded from the same source, each community action program was as different as its constituency. The local 10 percent share could come in the form of in-kind support—buildings, services, supplies, staff—rather than as a direct cash subsidy. A community might contribute its share in the form of office supplies and equipment or free school space for Head Start programs.

The funding, focus, and programs of these CAPs depended on the needs and abilities of the service area. The question of "community control" was a big one. The CAPs were to be run by people from within the community served, including public officials, members of civic groups, and representatives of the poor. Friction arose in some localities when local governments resented previously powerless segments of the community being given support that bypassed the existing power structure. Many city, county, and municipal governments assumed that the new organizations threatened the established political structure, and the degree of cooperation between local governments and the CAPs varied widely.

In some cases, the local government merely took over control of the CAP, perpetuating its existing policies (and occasionally its problems). In others, the community organizers battled with the local forces, creating ongoing conflicts and solving little. In the best instances, however, the CAPs worked hand in hand with regional governments to provide new services and augment existing programs.

At any rate, the local government could not prevent an eligible program from acquiring funds. The power vested in OEO was demonstrated early in the life of the agency when Alabama governor George Wallace vetoed a grant to a sharecropper cooperative in that state. OEO director Shriver, under his mandate from the president, was able to overrule the veto and disburse the funds in spite of state government objections.

Such a large, new, and enthusiastic organization was bound to make mistakes. Some allocations seemed unwise. For example, a few black militant political groups received large sums of OEO grant money. In other areas, power over the OEO funds was concentrated in the hands of local administrators, who perpetuated the status quo or skimmed the funds for other purposes.

In dry legislative language, the Economic Opportunity Act enunciated the theory that low-income people could attain the skills, knowledge, and motivations to become self-sufficient "if all available resources—public and private, federal and state, as well as local—were focused on this as a goal." The community action program was to concentrate on eliminating the causes of poverty. Such a program was defined as one that "includes or is designed to include a sufficient number of projects to provide, in sum, a range of services and activities having a measurable and potentially major impact on causes of poverty in the community."

As for the functions of community action agencies, the legislation identified these:

- planning systematically for and evaluating the program, including actions to develop information as to the problems and causes of poverty in the community, determine how much and how effectively assistance is being provided to deal with those problems and causes, and establish priorities among projects, activities and areas as needed for the best and most efficient use of resources;

- encouraging agencies engaged in activities related to the Community Action Program to plan for, secure and administer assistance available under this title or from other sources on a common or cooperative basis; providing planning or technical assistance to those agencies; and generally, in cooperation with community agencies and officials, undertaking actions to improve existing efforts to attack poverty, such as improving day-to-day communication, closing service gaps, focusing resources on the most needy, and improving additional opportunities to low-income individuals for regular employment or participation in the programs or activities for which those community agencies and officials are responsible;

- initiating and sponsoring projects responsive to needs of the poor which are not otherwise being met, with particular emphasis on providing central or common services that can be drawn upon by a variety of related programs, developing new approaches or new types of services that can be incorporated into other programs, and filling gaps pending the expansion or modification of those programs;

- establishing effective procedures by which the poor and area residents concerned will be enabled to influence the character of programs affecting their interests, providing for their regular participation in the implementation of those programs, and providing technical and other support needed to enable the poor and neighborhood groups to secure on their own behalf available assistance from public and private sources;

- joining with and encouraging business, labor and other private groups and organizations to undertake, together with officials and agencies, activities in support of the Community Action Program which will result in the additional use of private resources and capabilities, with a view to such activities as developing new employment opportunities, stimulating investment that will have a measurable impact in reducing poverty among residents of areas of concentrated poverty, and providing methods by which residents of those areas can work with private groups, firms and institutions in seeking solutions to problems of common concern.

Accomplishing all this was going to be a tall order. But the need was there, and within two years, some 1,000 community action agencies had been established across the country. Quite often they were given catchy names that could be reduced to punchy acronyms. And so it was that the war on poverty came to southwest Virginia as TAP.

Poverty in the Roanoke Valley

The Roanoke Valley is one of a series of valleys that lies in the natural basin between the Blue Ridge and Allegheny mountains. It is flanked by the Shenandoah Valley on the north and the New River Valley on the south. The Roanoke Valley proper includes only Roanoke County, which has three population concentrations—the cities of Roanoke and Salem and the town of Vinton—in its center. Although the TAP service area has expanded over the years to include territory not actually in the valley, the term "Roanoke Valley" is sometimes loosely used to refer to TAP's geographic target.

This area now includes the Fifth Planning District of Virginia (established in 1969)—Roanoke, Botetourt, Alleghany, and Craig counties and the cities of Roanoke, Salem, Covington, and Clifton Forge—as well as Rockbridge County and the cities of Lexington and Buena Vista, which are "uncapped," that is, not in the jurisdiction of any other community action agency. In addition, some of TAP's activities have taken it into Bedford, Montgomery, and Franklin counties and, ultimately, throughout the state and the southeastern region of the United States. "Today the Roanoke Valley, tomorrow the world" is an oft heard TAP slogan. Except for Craig County, TAP's service area lies within Virginia's Sixth Congressional District. This part of Virginia is almost a microcosm of the nation. Nearly 30 percent of the area's population live in rural areas, the other 70 percent in cities. Just over 10 percent of the people are black, the rest, primarily white. The topography includes both river bottoms—the James and Roanoke rivers traverse the area west to east—and mountaintops. The city of Roanoke has all the problems of Chicago, only on a smaller scale, and it has adjacent bedroom communities—Salem (mostly white collar) and Vinton (mostly blue collar). The area is heavily Protestant, but there are five Catholic churches and three Jewish synagogues in Roanoke. During the American bicentennial in 1976, the Canadian Broadcasting Corporation did a television special on a "typical" American community and several typical Americans. The community chosen was Lexington, in Rockbridge County; one of the typical Americans was a TAP outreach worker.

Historically, much of the development of the Roanoke Valley results from its location: this was the point where an Indian northwest trail and the east-west Trader's Path crossed. The city of Roanoke was actually settled in the middle of the eighteenth century, and because of its salt deposits, it carried the name of Big Lick. The community, however, languished for over a hundred years. An 1823 map of Virginia shows Salem, laid out in 1802, and Fincastle in Botetourt County, but not Roanoke. When Roanoke County was established out of Botetourt County territory in 1838, Salem, which had incorporated two years earlier, was chosen as the county seat. It became an independent city in 1968.

Big Lick rode the iron horse to prosperity in the late nineteenth century. It became a way station of the Virginia and

Tennessee (now Norfolk and Western) Railway in 1852, but it still had fewer than 700 people in 1882, when the Shenandoah Railway connected with the Virginia and Tennessee to provide a greater outlet for southwest Virginia coal. In two years, the population jumped to 5,000, and the burgeoning community became a chartered city, changing its name to Roanoke, an Indian word for money.

Vinton became an incorporated town the same year Roanoke became a city. Originally called Gish's Mill, the settlement had grown up with the coming of the railroad. The town was named Vinton after the Vinyard and Preston families, who, with the Gish family, owned most of the land in the area.

By the 1970 census, the broader Roanoke Valley region served by TAP had grown to over a quarter million people. By 1976, the city of Roanoke had a population of over 105,000, with much of the growth resulting from annexations of outlying areas. The suburbs, however, have continued to grow as well.

Population projections drawn from the city's 1976 base line call for an increased number of senior citizens (over 65) and adults in the work force (ages 34-64) but a smaller number of school-age children (ages 5-19) and young adults (ages 20-34). The non-white population is also expected to grow by the year 2000 from nearly 19,000 to over 25,000 (from 18 percent of the total population to 22 percent). It is also estimated that the productive population of the city (ages 20-64) will increase nearly 14 percent in the 1976-2000 period.

Although the Fifth Planning District includes the Roanoke metropolitan area, only 12 percent of the total land area is devoted to urban use, and much of the district is rural or not suitable for development. About 265,000 acres of land lie within the national forest system, and an additional 196,000 acres represent crop and pasture land.

The counties in the district but outside the Roanoke area

23

are not without economic potential. Botetourt is rich in mineral deposits and other natural resources. Alleghany County is one of Virginia's leading pulpwood producers, and its pulpwood is used principally by a large paper mill in Covington. Most of Craig County is forested; and although the entire county falls in the Jefferson National Forest region, the potential for increased pulpwood production is high. Also, the fertile land along the creeks in the county provides ample land for grain and livestock production.

Despite the growth and promise of the Roanoke area, the gloomy poverty statistics cited by President Johnson in 1964 were applicable in this area as well. In the Roanoke Valley, 23 percent of the families were poor. Over 80 percent of the poor families were white, but about 50 percent of the non-white families were poor. The percentage of poor families in the Roanoke Valley was slightly higher than the national percentage but slightly lower than for Virginia as a whole. The common standard for poverty at the time was an annual income of $3,000 for a family of four. In the Roanoke Valley, 13 percent of the families had incomes under $2,000. For the state of Virginia as a whole, 35 percent of the non-white families had annual incomes under $2,000.

For TAP, the precise poverty statistics were useful but not terribly important. The nameless poor that appeared on charts and bar graphs were people, and the problem would be approached in that light. This is the message carried by the fact sheet distributed by TAP as the agency girded for battle.

FACT: ⅓ of all the children in the Roanoke Valley
          came from poor families.
          These are children.
          They did not ask to be born.
          Shiftless, no-good, no-account, ignorant?
          No. Only *children*.

FACT: ¼ of ALL the families in the Roanoke
           Valley are poor.

           They have incomes of less than $3,000 a
           year.

           Many have incomes horrifyingly lower
           than that.

FACT: An education no higher than the 8th grade
           is *average* in Roanoke's poverty areas.

           A recent survey at schools in Roanoke
           poverty areas showed that average parents
           never got beyond the 8th grade.

           In at least one Roanoke school district, a
           5th grade education is the average.

Every % mark, every decimal point, every statistic
represents a living, breathing human being

           ...the man you spoke to on the street cor-
           ner this morning

           ...the child who misses school on the cold
           days because he has no clothing to wear

           ...the mother who does a day's work
           before she starts her day's job; the mother
           who farms out her children so she can have
           the privilege of working

TAP will carry the war on poverty into the
neighborhoods where poverty lives. The people who
will work in these programs, both for pay and for love,
are the people who will gain the most from the success of the programs.

TAP plans now to:

           ...provide day care for children of work-
           ing mothers and mothers who want to
           work but cannot because they are not free

           ...provide neighborhood centers, manned
           by neighborhood people, to keep children

off the streets and interested in worthwhile projects, and to help develop working skills and hobbies for senior citizens who want to be active again

...provide homemaking training: household budgeting, wise buying, nutrition, sewing, cooking ("...how can I make a decent meal out of *this*?")

...provide pre-vocational training for men with no jobs, fathers who have no skills and, therefore, no work

...provide reading and writing lessons for adult non-readers

...provide job counseling—how to look for jobs, how to get them

All this and more, to establish as many other *help-yourself* programs as are necessary in the Roanoke Valley to be sure that anyone who wants to help himself has the knowledge and the ability to do so with:

- more paying jobs
- more pre-school training for children
- more day care facilities for children, leaving parents free to work
- more reading and arithmetic for anyone who has not had it and wants to learn
- more knowledge of ways to have a clean, healthy home
- more pay and volunteer jobs
- more ways in which neighbors may help each other build a better way of life

TAP wants to make every statistic, every percentage point—that is, every single person—a producing productive human being, who is trained to make a decent living for himself and his family.

This is what the war on poverty is all about.

Enlist today.

Volunteer.

Think.

2

WARRIORS

I believe that those of us who do participate in society must figure out a way to help those who do not.

Cabell Brand, May 1979

NO ONE REALLY knew how to fight a war on poverty in 1965. To be sure, something had been learned from previous skirmishes with this age-old enemy, and some battles had been won, but earlier antipoverty measures—private charity and public welfare for the indigent, Social Security for the elderly—had largely dealt with symptoms. Community action agencies had been assigned the mission of engaging the enemy on all fronts, including his supply line, that is, the causes of poverty. The "front" was everywhere. And like a guerrilla war, the poverty war had to be fought amidst a populace that was often hostile. Many Americans did not believe that poverty was a problem; they distrusted federal programs that might force changes in local institutions. The national situation was further complicated in the South where the struggle against poverty became enmeshed with the civil-rights movement, which by the mid-1960s had turned more and more toward the "black power" ideology.

In this explosive environment, victory over poverty could not be won by good soldiers alone, people who dutifully executed well-conceived plans based on clearly established tactical principles. There *were* no clear plans and tactical principles. Instead, the battle required, in the classic sense, *warriors*—people who could lead as well as follow, make decisions quickly but decisively, adapt to the changing tides of battle, make friends among enemies, and "live off the land" when resources were scarce or supply or communications lines were cut. In short, community action required a breed of leadership different from that found in the established social service agencies.

The ministry proved to be a prominent source of such leadership. The black church had long been in the forefront of social struggle and had little difficulty in fusing poverty and discrimination as related adversaries, if not actually the same foe. The white churches, particularly the Protestant denominations, agonized more in this regard. In general, they had become part of the social establishment. Not surprisingly, then, those who came from the pulpit to the poverty war turned out to be religious mavericks, prophets not honored in, and often not honoring, their own land.

"We're not only concerned with dollars," Bristow Hardin claimed. "We're not only concerned with job skills, which are still dollars. We're concerned with building bridges. We must drop the professional claptrap which allows us to be dispassionate helpers of the poor. We must somehow renew our passion—our dedication toward people." These words were repeated again and again as Hardin spoke to churches and civic organizations, drumming up community backing for TAP.

In many places, CAP agencies were perceived as homes for misfits and malcontents, and some fit the description. They rejected the establishment and warred against it, figuratively shedding blood as necessary. And most of their victories were Pyrrhic. More successful were the CAAs that managed to bridge the gap between the advantaged and the disadvantaged, to find support in the traditionally skeptical business community, to count success in terms of missions accomplished rather than martyrs sacrificed.

While cautioning that the theme should not be played too loudly, most historians today believe that personality can be a historical force, that social outcomes are not totally the result of events over which people have no control. From this perspective, it can be said that the quality of a community action program has often been determined by the quality of its warriors. TAP brought together an unlikely group of people, but they proved to have the quality necessary for a successful effort. In the long list of TAP warriors, four people stand out as leaders who made things happen. They are Cabell Brand, Bristow Hardin, Ted Edlich, and Georgia Meadows.

Cabell Brand

Cabell (rhymes with rabble) Brand says that his greatest claim to fame is that he is a descendant, albeit illegitimate, of Thomas Jefferson. It seems that Mr. Jefferson, who was among other things a lawyer, provided legal counsel to the Cabell family. Apparently, he visited the household more than his professional obligations required, for he fathered a child out of wedlock. Cabell even inherited the Jeffersonian red hair, although it has since been overtaken by gray.

This story may be apocryphal, but there is no question that Cabell's roots in the Roanoke Valley stretch back several generations and qualify him for membership in the local establishment. Born in Salem in 1923, Cabell grew up in the Great Depression and felt some of the pains of hard times. But there was always food to eat at the Brand home on College Avenue, and good times eventually returned.

Cabell followed the family tradition of attending Virginia Military Institute in nearby Lexington, and when World War II intervened, he put in four years as an army officer. He returned to VMI to complete his degree in electrical engineering and then took a job as a State Department officer, a position that landed him in Berlin during the Blockade of 1948.

It is not difficult to imagine Cabell as a diplomat. Tall

30

and trim, he has a manner that is usually decribed as court-
ly and a style that is as warm as it is charming. His speech
flows with the ''oots'' and ''aboots'' that are characteristic
of the Virginia gentleman. Seated in his study, with three-
piece suit and delicately balanced demitasse, he might today be ambassador to the Court of St. James.

But business, not diplomacy, was to be his way of life
after 1949. The Brand family had operated a shoe business
since 1904. Originally called the Brand Shoe Company, the
name was later changed to Ortho-Vent Shoe Company (after
the type of shoe that was sold) and then to Stuart McGuire
Company, the name it has today. It is characteristic of
Cabell's approach to business that despite his concern for
family tradition, the name ''Stuart McGuire'' has no family
connection at all; it simply tested well in a market survey.

When Cabell took over the business from his father, he
stopped the liquidation that was in process and started to
build the small company into a major enterprise. On the
basis of its door-to-door business (mostly shoes, but now
clothing and jewelry also), Stuart McGuire now has multi-
million dollar gross sales, hundreds of employees, and
thousands of other people who work as company sales
agents. Although the company is now public, the Brand
family has the controlling stock interest, and Cabell is the
company president.

The Brand home on College Avenue is large, handsome,
and tastefully decorated with hundreds of valuable *objets
d'art*. Cabell and his wife, Shirley, have traveled extensively,
and Cabell's office, like his home, suggests a man of varied
tastes and interests. He is equally comfortable discussing
the marketing of shoes, philosophy, Chinese culture, poverty, or the American economy. He is a thoughtful man who
is able to grapple with the most cosmic issues while still dealing effectively with the day-to-day details of life and work.
And he is totally committed to community action and to
TAP.

There is little question that the world of small business is an unlikely place to find recruits for the poverty war. For most small-business men, the community action program meant higher taxes, higher minimum wages, and threats to business independence. It took an exceptional businessman to see that helping the poor would serve the interest of business in the long run. Cabell Brand is exceptional.

Always extremely active in civic affairs, Cabell was a member of the Roanoke Valley Council of Community Services in 1964 when word of the war on poverty first drifted into the area. At a meeting of the council, a gentleman, who shall remain nameless, rose to denounce the war on poverty and, in so doing, helped to speed its advance into the Roanoke Valley. Cabell disagreed with the man philosophically and decided that if this gentleman were against the antipoverty movement, then he, Cabell, would probably be for it.

Cabell obtained a copy of the Economic Opportunity Act and analyzed it thoroughly; he studied congressional hearings and staff reports; he went to Washington and talked to Sargent Shriver. He concluded that the antipoverty program was urgently needed in the Roanoke area.

Cabell was scheduled to make a speech before the prestigious Roanoke Valley Torch Club on May 11, 1965. He dropped his planned speech on computers and decided to talk about the poverty program. Since "Cabell's Torch Club speech" has come to be regarded locally as a major factor in bringing community action to Roanoke, some excerpts seem appropriate. Cabell first dehorned the Economic Opportunity Act by presenting it as a continuation of enlightened American traditions:

> Just what is this poverty war? Is it another step toward socialism? Is it just something to get votes because it is politically popular to wage a war to help the poor?
>
> The Economic Opportunity Act of 1964, more commonly called the Poverty Bill, is just one in a series of bills stretch-

ing back to the Social Security law which Roosevelt signed 30 years ago, designed to raise the floor under the standard of living of those groups in our population who are less able to help themselves.

He then put the bill in the broadest contexts, national prosperity and international peace.

As I view it, the basic purpose of this type of legislation is a great deal more than just to help the poor. I view it as economic legislation rather than social legislation. I believe that most of these new laws, if properly handled, can help solve two of our most fundamental problems—the solutions for which are in everybody's interest—Democrats, Republicans, chambers of commerce, National Association of Manufacturers, labor unions, the business community, and most of all, the citizens of this country.

The first of these two problems is the international problem. This is the political problem of trying to prevent a nuclear war without backing down or compromising on the fundamental principle of self-determination for ourselves and the free countries of the world.

The second problem is a national problem, primarily an economic one, of keeping our country growing, creating enough new opportunities to absorb the rising labor force, adjusting to the population explosion so that our standard of living here continues to improve without cyclical depressions. If we had a depression and could not afford the defenses required to protect ourselves, we could lose the international political problem.

On the other hand, it is my contention that if we not only solve the national economic problems, but can accelerate our economic activity and increase our economic strength, we might solve the international political problem in our contest with the Soviet Union.

Then came the "everyone benefits" argument that conservative businessmen would accept:

This may sound like utopia, but this is the way economic strength works. The greater the standard of living, the greater the purchasing power of one segment of the economy, the greater benefits accrue to other segments. In trade, everyone benefits: the people who are trading for what they want, the people who receive what they want in return, the profits that are made from this economic activity—a substantial share of which goes to the various governments to give them the resources to do their work.

By giving people an opportunity to help themselves— whether, in initial stages, it's food to give them strength, health to give them the ability, education to give them the opportunity, or whatever else is required to give them the hope—everyone benefits.

Cabell concluded with a ringing endorsement of the war on poverty as a sound investment:

In a democracy the human being is the most important element. His dignity as a human being, his ability to satisfy his basic needs for health, frugal comfort, and moral living at a decent level, is a minimum requirement for collective survival.

Most references to poverty have been made in the context of low income or lack of financial resources. But our war on poverty begins in the mind. We think, we create, we produce, and we prosper—and in that order.

Our success economically and, I submit, politically will be determined by the success of our investment in our people.

Cabell's Torch Club speech helped to galvanize action by the local authorities. With Dave Herbert, executive director of the Roanoke Valley Council of Community Services, and Cabell leading the way, support was obtained from the city of Roanoke and the counties of Roanoke and Botetourt. An organization was formed to apply for funding from the Office of Economic Opportunity (OEO). Funding—first a planning grant and later a grant for a day-care center program—was soon forthcoming, and TAP was in business. Cabell was named president of the board of directors, a position he still holds. An old flour mill on Shenandoah Avenue was converted into a headquarters building, and the board began to search for staff.

For the key position of executive director, the board interviewed 25 people. In a split decision, the nod went to Bristow Hardin. Hired at the same time were Osborne Payne, a black educator, and Sam Barone, who had experience in teaching the physically disabled. Payne had just returned from Liberia, where he had helped establish rural schools; Barone came from Richmond. Hardin was local.

Bristow Hardin

Bristow's background clearly marked him as a maverick warrior. He was related to the famed gunfighter John Wesley Hardin; his ancestors had both ridden with Quantrill and marched with Sherman in the Civil War. He took a bachelor's degree at William and Mary, then a master's degree in drama from the University of Texas. Bristow's brief fling at an acting career in New York City was unsuccessful, and he began teaching to feed his growing family.

In 1965, Bristow was the principal of West End Elementary School in Roanoke and also the educational television coordinator for the city school system. He was already a controversial figure. His fight for racial integration in the schools had made him quite a few enemies, but even his friends regarded him as a somewhat strange school principal. Wilma Warren, who worked with Bristow at West End and followed him to TAP, recalled the West End days in a memorial issue of the TAP newsletter published after his death in 1975:

> The first time John Sabean's son David met Bristow, he said, "Daddy, is Mr. Hardin really your boss? Is he really the head of TAP?" "Yes, son, he is," John replied. "It's hard to believe," said David, shaking his head.
>
> When I worked for Bristow at West End School, I saw visitors shaking their heads with the same disbelief.

35

Bristow never forgot what it was like to be a little kid cooped up in a classroom. At the end of a long, rainy day, he would go into classrooms and challenge the teacher to a duel with long cardboard tubes. While the children stood back and cheered, Bristow and the teacher would jump over desks and charge at each other down the aisles shouting "En garde!" and "Touche!" When Bristow won—which was nearly always—he would make the pupils beg him to show mercy and spare their teacher from being expelled from school.

There wasn't a student at West End School who didn't know that the worst thing you could do was lie to Mr. Hardin—or that the wooden pinwheel he kept in his desk was a lie detector in his hands—amazingly, it would spin *backwards* when anyone told a lie.

The next worst thing was to shoot first in a watergun battle. Bristow kept an arsenal of loaded waterguns in his desk, along with the lie detector, and he showed no mercy to anyone foolish enough to take him on.

Edna Williams, the sixth-grade teacher, and I tried one day to ambush Bristow with a watergun. While Bristow always fought with all rules suspended, he was outraged when we did. He rushed back into his office, grabbed two guns, and in five minutes Edna and I were soaked. To prevent further rebellions, he had the morning school patrols, just coming in, stand formation as he stripped us for our guns.

Bristow's style of leadership did not change when he became the top man at TAP. On the contrary, with a larger stage on which to play, he gave an even fuller rein to his unorthodox leadership tendencies. As a result, "Bristow stories" abound in the Roanoke Valley. Wilma again:

When Bristow became TAP's executive director, I thought he might decide to take himself seriously, but I should have known better. He was an unorthodox administrator, and he could never see himself as a big shot. He loved to answer his own phone with a booming "Bristow." He once told a new switchboard operator, who only knew a "Mr. Hardin" who worked at TAP, "This is Bristow! Just say 'yes'!"

He taught us his basic principles of management by lecture and example. "Never make an enemy unnecessarily," he would warn, and he would apologize to a potential enemy for an error in judgment. "Never lie to the press," he would instruct us, and those of us who would have known know that he never did.

Bristow never expected himself or TAP to be perfect, so he didn't try to impress the many visitors who came from Washington or Philadelphia or Richmond to evaluate us. Long-term friendships developed with most of them, but occasionally one of them would try to impress Bristow with his expertise or power. On these occasions, he would fall asleep and snore loudly, leaving the rest of us to carry on. If we were willing to suffer fools, that was our business, but he certainly was not.

Nothing made Bristow angrier than having to talk to three secretaries to get to some bureaucrat on the phone. His stock reply to "May I say who is calling?" was "God," and it usually got him through right away. One unusually officious interceptor persisted, "I beg your pardon, who?" to which Bristow shouted, "God! G-O-D!" The unruffled voice said sweetly, "And what may I tell Mr. Jones you are calling about?" "Sex! S-E-X!" bellowed Bristow at this outrageous abuse of power.

He enjoyed playing travel agent for us, often routing us a hundred miles out of our way to a favorite restaurant or campground. If you returned from a trip without taking his advice, he never let you forget it.

Traveling to meetings with Bristow was a prize fringe benefit for TAP staffers. His appreciation for nature's wonders was profound, and with his sharp eyes he saw many things the rest of us missed. "Look, look, look!" he would shout at the sight of calves playfully butting heads in a distant field, or of a long sentinel of a tree standing watch over the countryside. "God," he would breathe when we came upon some unexpected gift of nature, "do you know how lucky we are to live in Virginia? It's got everything—the mountains, the shore, and everything in between. God, we're lucky!''

Heads shook in disbelief in Washington, Richmond, or anywhere Bristow went in the early days of TAP. His sheer size and loud voice caused some people to dismiss him as a character; other were worn down by his persistence and capitulated to his viewpoint. But for most people he dealt with, Bristow became a legend. He could always be counted on to cut through the bull with some earthy phrase and turn a boring meeting into a lively human event.

One memorable morning at a meeting on Afton Mountain, Bristow called everyone whose room faced east (and, by mistake, several whose didn't) to get up and see the sunrise. He was like a child at Christmas, and when I recall that morning, I think of a song Bristow liked to sing:

One man can awaken another,
The second can arouse his next-door brother.
The three can rouse a town
By turning the whole place upside down.
The many awake can make such a fuss
That it finally awakens the rest of us.
One man up with dawn in his eyes...multiplies.

Another frequently told story is usually called "The Day Bristow Saved the Bull." As told by Ted Edlich, who was there, Bristow attended a bullfight in Acapulco. When the time came to decide whether the bull should be dispatched with the matador's sword, the crowd was virtually unanimous in cheering the matador on. But not Bristow; *he* rose to cheer for the bull. At first, he was a lone voice; then a few others nearby joined in, and soon the tide was turned. The bull was spared, thus supporting Bristow's belief that a few energized people can make almost anything happen.

Most of the people who remember Bristow today do so fondly. Osborne Payne describes him as a "jovial, *rotundant*" person who was a brilliant conversationalist and a good listener, a master at getting things done through others. Payne, now a Baltimore businessman, was a suit-and-tie man himself, but he came to accept Bristow's informal dress and manner. "Clean, sloppy, and grinning" was the image he projected to Payne.

But there are others who see Bristow in a somewhat different light. One of them is Ralph Leach. Leach was fairly typical of the maverick ministers who joined the antipoverty movement. While rector at an Episcopal church in Louisville in the 1960s, he participated in a number of anti-Vietnam and open housing demonstrations. Consequently, Leach spent some time in jail in the company of such men as Ralph Abernathy and the brother of Martin Luther King, Jr. The bishop decided that perhaps Leach should ply his skills elsewhere, and he came to TAP in 1969, serving until 1973 as manpower director.

While noting that Bristow was "fantastic, charismatic, and amiable," Leach feels that he also could be "arbitrary, capricious, despotic, and, on occasion, devastatingly cruel." Leach cites several incidents that demonstrate this side of Bristow's nature. Once Leach and Bristow had a disagreement over some manpower matter. John Sabean, then head of the Opportunities Industrialization Council that TAP had created, agreed with Leach and wrote a careful memorandum to Bristow supporting his position. Bristow wrote back: "I have received your memorandum [of such and such date]. When I want your advice, you will know because I will say, 'John, may I have your advice?' " Another time at a staff meeting, a woman questioned whether TAP was becoming too institutionalized. Bristow bristled at the suggestion, suppressed all discussion of the matter, and, in Leach's words, "barred her from all meetings of the inner sanctum for months."

The "inner sanctum," whose members were never defined, was a source of some dispute at TAP. Leach refers to this in support of his assertion that Bristow was mostly

a "small democrat" but also somewhat "demagogic."
Writes Leach:

> There had been some extended and somewhat heated
> discussion about personnel practices—Bristow's position
> was that those in his inner circle could pretty much do as
> they pleased because what they would do would be right and
> good, but that others had to be closely circumscribed by
> rules. Jim Jones had disagreed vehemently—and later I
> typed notes of my own thoughts on the matter, to help me
> set forth my own position to Bristow. As I recall, the set-
> ting forth never came off; I think I started one day but he
> quickly made it clear he wasn't interested in hearing any
> more contrary opinions on the subject.

All involved seem to agree on one point: Bristow's drive
was a major factor in TAP's success, and he established an
espirit de corps in the organization that gave it direction after
his death.

Ted Edlich

Bristow Hardin was a tough act to follow. Theodore J.
Edlich III, the chosen successor, always seems bland by com-
parison. While Bristow roared his disapprovals, Ted's
displeasure is more likely to be registered in an increasing
glint to his steely blue eyes. (Wilma Warren says that after
one look at Ted's eyes, she implored Bristow to hire the
young man.) Where Bristow intuited truth, Ted is more likely
to quote Kurt Vonnegut or a passage from books like
Megatrends. Where Bristow reveled in intellectual disorder,
Ted conceptualizes the various universes he encounters.
Where Bristow managed by charisma, Ted imposes management systems.

Ironically, Ted's attempt to streamline management
created a major staff crisis. Several years after taking over
as executive director, he reshuffled the staff to bring greater
accountability to the operating departments. One effect of
the reshuffling was the elimination of the position of depu-

ty director, a spot held by Charlene Chambers, who had some partisans on the board of directors and among the senior staff. Ted's action was upheld by the TAP board by a two-to-one majority, however.

In most other ways, Ted is very much a Hardin disciple. He believes in hiring people, not filling slots, and he stresses output over procedures. He is something of a B. F. Skinner in supporting the notion that people work because of the rewards they expect to receive. If crime pays, then people become criminals.

Like Cabell and Bristow, Ted comes from a privileged background. A child of New York City (1 Fifth Avenue), Ted turned to religion to find greater meaning in life than he found in the streets of Gotham. After graduating from Union Theological Seminary and Yale Divinity School, he became the Presbyterian minister in the small town of Buchanan, Virginia. He was there whan TAP was established. Although Ted defied many traditions of rural Virginia, for example, marrying black couples in a white church, he managed to get along well with the elders. "They were good people: they treated me right," says Ted. Later, he took a job with Montgomery Presbytery and worked closely with the TAP program.

Ted joined the TAP staff in 1968. He directed the Head Start program, worked in community organization, and then took charge of the Human Services Training and Technical Assistance division. Given his excellent record over the years with TAP, his succession to the executive directorship in 1975 came as no surprise.

Quieter than Bristow, but no less committed to the poor, Ted led the attack on new areas of need such as ex-offenders, reclaimed and reorganized the water project, which had been operating outside TAP, and continued to push TAP forward as a leader in the CAP world.

That world Ted sees as the best hope for the nation's disadvantaged people. In 1978, Ted sent a paper to the White

House, urging the creation of a cabinet-level Department of Human Rights in which community action agencies would play a major role. He has peppered congressional committees with similar recommendations.

The failure of others to act on his far-reaching recommendations has not lessened Ted's passion for reform, his inability "to digest the horrors of this world." He argues that world pressures will ultimately force the United States to address the question of human inequality because there will be a world poverty crisis, not just a domestic crisis. At the moment, however, "we have sold our souls to the petro-auto-industrial complex and are preying on the rest of the world." It is a clarion call to action, not a cry of despair.

Georgia Meadows

A concerned businessman, a disenchanted educator, a minister with a mission—these are the people who have been most in the public eye in the war on poverty in the Roanoke Valley. But behind them has marched an army of community residents, volunteers mostly, who had lived with poverty and discrimination when Bristow was studying acting and Ted was in the seminary and Cabell was building up his business. No one exemplifies this largely unsung group better than Georgia Meadows.

She has celebrated her golden wedding anniversary and must, therefore, be in the vicinity of age 70. But Georgia's mahogany face could pass for 35, and she is more spirited intellectually than most of today's teen-agers. Nor has she ever lost her sense of humor. At a TAP-produced "Gong Show," when Ted sallied forth on "Danny Boy" or some such, it was Georgia who gave the gong to her close friend and frequent traveling companion.

It is a testament to the strength of Georgia Meadows that Botetourt County, which adjoins Roanoke County, became part of the TAP service area. Like most of the outlying areas in the valley, the county was suspicious of community action and ill-disposed to make local-share financial contributions.

Georgia was born near Fincastle, the county seat, and has lived her entire life in Botetourt County. A graduate of Virginia State College, she also studied at Columbia, the University of Virginia, Northwestern, and Harvard, all the while remaining anchored as a teacher in the local public school system. Says Georgia: "I guess I could have gotten a job anywhere, but I didn't want to leave Botetourt. I just used the knowledge to become a better teacher."

One of her threshold problems as a teacher was making sure all the children could spell and pronounce the name of the county. It was named for an Englishman, Lord Botetourt, whose strange Norman moniker was a puzzlement to the children of the twentieth century. (It sounds like body-tot.) But most of her 48 years in the public school system were spent trying to inspire "her children" to greatness.

An activist in the Botetourt Improvement Association and many other local civic and church organizations, Georgia Meadows was a natural for the TAP board of directors, and she served in this capacity for a number of years. Georgia now calls the period of board service one of the "nicer experiences" of her retirement years.

She gave strong support to Ted's initiatives and often accompanied him on out-of-town forays to gain support for the community action program. At TAP, she enjoyed the "beehive" atmosphere, the sense of involvement in a self-help effort, and the training sessions that were held for board members. Most importantly, she appreciated the opportunity she had been given to continue her work on behalf of her community. Georgia Meadows was not ready to retire to a rocking chair and contemplate the blue "gazing ball" that sits in her front yard.

The community workers like Georgia have been the key

to TAP's success. They translate TAP's programs into language the community can understand. And some translation has been required, given TAP's unorthodox habits.

The TAP Style

The rambling, multi-story building that is TAP's headquarters is full of odd corners and strangely shaped offices, and the unorthodox building attracted an unorthodox crowd of people. TAP staffers wore jeans and T-shirts and decorated their offices with posters. Although this was not particularly unusual elsewhere in the country during the 1960s, it seemed strange enough to the local residents. Initially the young poverty warriors were distrusted by local residents. Hardin added to the eccentric overtones of the organization by using profanity, wearing "casual" clothes, and generally maintaining the same approach that had earned him his reputation as a wacko school principal.

To a certain extent, the kind of work TAP was doing required a new approach and an unorthodox style. Those who worked with the poor needed a heightened sensitivity to the unspoken problems of their clients. For example, a crucial aspect of poverty assistance proved to be training the poor to live with and relate to other people. Those who had never been employed had to learn how to look for a job and how to behave in an interview. They even needed lessons in hygiene, so they would know to wash before reporting to work.

Hardin embraced "sensitivity training" as part of the TAP philosophy. TAP staffers participated in workshops, trying to become sensitized to the needs of poor people and sensitive in addressing them. Encounter sessions and psychodramas took place in a conference room with the participants seated on brightly colored pillows.

For a while the conference room was only accessible

through Bristow Hardin's office. It had no door, and entrance was through a low hole in the wall. Hardin felt that getting on one's hands and knees before a meeting was a humbling experience, and that entering the conference room in this way meant that things could be conducted on a more equal and unpretentious basis. Not that Hardin cared for meetings much; he was known to fall asleep, sometimes audibly, when he felt things had gotten dull or pointless.

The "TAP style" was hardly welcomed by the local business community. It is, after all, difficult for someone who wears a suit and tie to feel that a laid-back, blue-denimed, long-haired poverty worker is actually accomplishing anything useful. "Those hippies at TAP" dealt with the criticism as best they could; the clothing question, at least, was justifiable. An important aspect of counseling is trust, and it is easier for a client to trust a peer. TAP's credibility with its constituency was undoubtedly helped by the fact that nobody on the staff looked like a banker. The same style that hurt TAP with the establishment helped TAP with its service community.

The Racial Issue

TAP's policy of racial equality also came under fire, and from both sides of the fence. Hardin's stated aim was to ignore questions of color when it came to selecting qualified people for staff positions. TAP's personnel roster was racially balanced, but the fact that the power structure followed traditional lines, which favored whites, offended some civil rights groups. And the fact that the head of TAP was a white man angered black power advocates, who felt that TAP's energies should be more strongly directed toward the black community. Even though TAP's staff was at least 50 percent black, some hard-liners felt that a black person should head the organization.

45

Hardin and the TAP staff countered these accusations by pointing out that although half of the black population in the Roanoke Valley was poor, 80 percent of the poor people in the valley were white. The vast majority of people that TAP was trying to reach and help were white, and it was counterproductive to superimpose racial considerations on TAP's aims.

In meetings with black groups, Hardin was firm in his adherence to principles of equal rights, equal opportunity, and shared responsibility, but he was also firm in his defense of his right to keep his job. TAP continued to hire blacks, share power with black groups, and assist members of black communities, but it remained white-run and white-directed.

TAP's personnel policies led to unintentional discrimination, however. At one point, it became clear that black TAP employees were earning substantially less, on the average, than white TAP employees. TAP's policy of hiring people at salaries that were a percentage of their pay before joining TAP had inadvertently perpetuated the discrimination and wage differentiation that went on in the normal economic community. Pay scales and salary policies were rapidly changed to eliminate the disparity, but the sense of injustice was hard to overcome.

TAP's outreach programs, however, helped maintain racial harmony in its service area. One oft-repeated example of Hardin's ability to deal peacefully, firmly, and fairly with black groups came after the assassination of Martin Luther King, Jr. in 1968. While the rest of the country was rioting, a group of blacks came to TAP, threatening to "march and shed blood."

Hardin agreed that marching was a fine idea; he could understand why they wanted to do it, but felt they should march and shed blood in a way of which Dr. King would have approved. As a consequence, demonstrators staged a protest march under banners that read "Blood for a King." Led by Hardin and other TAP staffers, the march wound through Roanoke before ending up at the blood bank, where dozens of pints were given in Martin Luther King's memory.

TAP literally came under fire from whites for espousing integrationist policies. A TAP retreat in Franklin County was attacked by shotgun-wielding white militants protesting against such interracial fraternization. But in a community with deep-seated racist roots (some of the fiercest battles over integration were fought in Virginia), TAP walked a tightrope between white supremacy and black power.

An Evaluation of TAP

When TAP began, it had no experienced staff members, no experts, and few precedents to follow from previous community action programs. It grew rapidly and erratically and learned to cope with problems as they arose. This has led over the years to internal difficulties or to growing pains, depending on one's perspective.

The question of poverty representation in TAP's management arose early in the history of the organization. Government guidelines for community action programs called for broad-based community participation; TAP's original charter called for poor members of the community to be elected to the board of directors.

But the poor community members originally on the board of directors were chosen by the TAP board itself. In order to allow the community to select its own representatives, the TAP bylaws were changed in 1966 to provide positions on the board of directors for "representatives of the poor." A board member, A. Byron Smith, disagreed with the change, charging that a "representative of the poor" need not be a poor person. The rest of the board maintained that the change enabled TAP area's low-income residents to choose their own board members. Smith resigned in protest, but the change remained.

Smith remained critical of TAP. In 1969, as an officer of the NAACP, he requested that TAP provide the NAACP with information regarding the parents of Head Start enrollees. TAP provided information on its own staff, but maintained that Head Start records were confidential. Smith set up an NAACP committee to investigate TAP, but no wrongdoing was found.

TAP's controversial public image opened the organization to criticism from area governments and citizens. There were rumors of illegal activities at TAP centers; these proved to be unfounded. When a married couple embezzled money from TAP's operating funds, the subsequent investigation found the bookkeeping system to be adequate and the organization not at fault. Almost all cases of malfeasance involving TAP proved to be unrelated to the management practices of the organization. In spite of public criticism, TAP continued to persevere and expand.

In order to dispel some of the questions about TAP, the Roanoke Valley Council of Community Services acquired in 1968 a $50,000 grant to evaluate TAP. The council hired Greenleigh Associates, a Washington area consulting firm, to investigate TAP and present a report of its conclusions. Greenleigh's investigators spent seven months talking to TAP staff, Roanoke Valley residents, and local administrators to gather information about TAP's effectiveness. Surprisingly enough to many people, the report was favorable.

> Since its establishment, TAP has become a large-scale organization in a relatively short period of time. It has developed its administration, structure, staff, programs, and strategies rapidly and with a minimum of direction or guidance from the Federal government. Many of its programs represent drastic departures from traditional ways of delivering services.... TAP has, on occasion, become the focus of controversy.

The report pointed out the unique factors that should be considered in relation to TAP's function in the community, including TAP's "relative newness" and its "exceedingly rapid rate of growth," the constantly fluctuating federal government policies and erratic funding, and staffing difficulties. The report noted that the "community action agency is necessarily dealing with sensitive areas, frequently fraught with conflict and controversy, which may touch upon issues basic to the life of the community."

The Greenleigh report made a number of critical points, but its overall tone was positive. "TAP has had a significant impact in the Roanoke Valley," the report began.

In those geographical "target areas" where TAP has concentrated its efforts, it has reached a significantly large proportion of residents, most of whom feel that TAP has helped the community. This consumer acceptance was found in both white and Negro neighborhoods, and it is a clear indication that TAP programs are, in general, reaching those whom the antipoverty program was designed to serve. There was also some evidence that TAP, in reaching and working with some of the more militant Negro youth, was a significant positive force in averting racial disturbances. . . . The poor have begun, with TAP assistance, to become organized and to participate more directly in the affairs of local government. . . .

The study revealed no evidence of incitement of poverty-area groups by TAP staff. TAP workers were, on the contrary, most consistent in advocating legitimate channels of expression to all groups, including those who might be considered dangerously hostile.

The Greenleigh report did find problems in the TAP organizational structure, however. "It is important that TAP strengthen its administration and operation in order to consolidate and improve the variety of programs it has accomplished in the past few years." The report also criticized several TAP programs individually, recommending that some be spun off to local jurisdictions, some be consolidated, and some be scrapped.

Greenleigh Associates recommended a total restructuring of TAP's administration and suggested delegating "to other agencies programs and functions which can be operated by other agencies, eliminating those programs and activities which are not effective, and generally strengthening the overall administration and staff supportive functions."

In addition to the evaluation of TAP itself, Greenleigh Associates performed a household interview study to measure TAP's effectiveness in reaching the poor. Members of 230 households in Roanoke, Salem, Vinton, and Dundee were interviewed.

TAP's outreach to its constituency proved to be consistent and excellent; according to the study, "Ninety-five percent of the respondents said they had heard of TAP, and 45 percent reported they had been contacted by a TAP program representative at one time."

Thirty-seven percent of the respondents reported that TAP had helped either them personally or a member of their family. Eighty-two percent of those interviewed thought that TAP was helping the community. Both blacks and whites responded favorably to questions about TAP, proving that the TAP programs were not segregated or directed solely at one segment of the poor population.

After the Greenleigh report was completed, the Citizens Anti-Poverty Programs Evaluation Committee of the Roanoke Valley Council of Community Services used it as a basis for its own study of TAP. The committee's results were similar to those of the Greenleigh study. "The Committee is of the opinion that Total Action Against Poverty has been more than adequate in carrying out its program. . . . The Committee feels that the program as a whole has considerable merit and is one which in most of its aspects should be retained as an integral and necessary part of the Roanoke Valley."

The committee also found TAP "responsible as any

organization, individual, or group for the peaceful racial atmosphere that has prevailed in the Valley.''

Although the general findings of the citizens' committee agreed with those of the Greenleigh report, the committee recommended a more wide-ranging reorganization and suggested a two-step program for meeting this goal. Like the Greenleigh report, the committee identified communication and organizational problems within each of the specific TAP program areas.

TAP was successfully reorganized along the lines suggested by the committee's report, although the perpetual scramble for funds made this process difficult.

Relations with the Salem government became strained when the city of Salem decided not to renew Cabell Brand's appointment to the TAP board of directors. Brand was not notified of the change until it was nearly a fait accompli, and his designated replacement was unaware of the circumstances regarding his nomination.

TAP's supporters rallied behind Brand and insisted that since he had been elected by the entire board and had the most experience in working with TAP, he should be reappointed. Brand was duly reinstated on the TAP board of directors and remains the only chairman it has ever had.

Over the years, financial problems continued to plague TAP; as the war in Vietnam grew hotter, the war on poverty cooled off, and federal funds grew increasingly difficult to obtain. Nimble grantsmanship by the TAP staff kept the organization afloat, although at one point there was no money at all in the TAP treasury. Local governments increased their contributions to TAP, and private foundations, such as the Ford Foundation, were recruited for funds. TAP turned some programs over to branches of local governments or separate agencies, while other programs were consolidated or dropped. Somehow, TAP managed to meet the payroll and keep the services going.

3

TOTAL ACTION
AGAINST POVERTY

*Why not build all our programs on families? We could iden-
tify problems—lack of job skills, the father is an offender.
Total action should be based on families.*

Charlene Chambers, October 1979

IN THE WORLD of the planners, personnel and financial
resources are allocated to programs in accordance with
established priorities, and the programs are carefully directed
at achieving goals and objectives. The reports that community action agencies submit to funding sources reflect this
thinking, but the reports rarely describe the reality. In reality,
actions are launched against targets of opportunity.

TAP is no exception. It is—and always has been—a guerrilla army flailing away at the enemy wherever found.
Whatever is lacking in terms of grand strategy has been made
up for by enthusiasm for the battle. Thus the name "total
action against poverty" has proved an apt choice because
it describes the organization's modus operandi.

The list of programs conducted by TAP in the 18 years
of its existence is encyclopedic and spans practically every
aspect of the human condition. There have been programs
to provide food, clothing, shelter, medical care, education,
and spiritual comfort to people of all ages and races and
walks of life.

The specific items on the list change over the years as
available funds ebb and flow and as the perception of needs

varies. In the beginning was Head Start (preschool education); today there is Virginia CARES (an ex-offender program); and in between, TAP has tried everything imaginable
to take action against poverty.

Program Development

TAP has always been a program development agency, trying a wide variety of new, different, and personal approaches
to poverty eradication. Simply because a program idea had
never been tried before was never a deterrent. If a problem
seemed to call for an unorthodox solution, the TAP staff
was only too willing to try it. It would be unrealistic to say
that such innovative programs were invariably roaring suc-
cesses, but it is true that though some ultimately flopped,
others went on to expand and become autonomous.

TAP has always focused on development, rather than
maintenance, and program autonomy is one of TAP's goals.
The TAP philosophy states that a successful program should
stand on its own or be administered through a local agency
that has responsibility for that area of service. Such TAP-
initiated projects as swimming pools, family-planning services, alcohol-counseling services, and senior citizens services
have all been spun off to other agencies or local
governments.

TAP has not abandoned its original goals, however. The
first annual report described TAP's three basic programs:

1. For children—to help them get ready for and complete
public schooling. 2. For adults—to train them for better
jobs. 3. For each person, each family living in poverty—to
help them help themselves become productive members of
society. TAP has very few jobs to offer. TAP has no handouts, no welfare. But TAP offers hope, education, and
training. . . .

TAP believes that much of the answer to the problem of
poverty can be found in sound research, education, and

community-wide facing of facts. TAP believes that we should offer a man a helping hand rather than a "handout." If TAP gives away anything, it is hope and opportunity.

The number of employees actually working on programs has varied over the years; TAP's staff hit a high of 415 in 1969 and a low of 176 in 1973. However, in spite of budget reductions, TAP has continued to expand and improve the range of services available to the poor of the Roanoke Valley and the Fifth Planning District.

In its first 18 months of operation, TAP expanded rapidly to include eight basic programs. From this original eight, many others grew and developed. Some were spun off to other agencies; others were dropped or expanded and diversified.

The motivating force behind each new TAP program must be a definite need within the community. As the TAP program development manual states:

Far too many efforts take place without a solid identification of need.... Counselors attempt to cure people without firmly establishing the problem. Businesses establish sales plans and strategies without adequate market research. People of good will begin community programs and institutions often because they sound good.

The most important key to real community change is the establishment of a real and perceived need.... That is, it is important that the need reflect something that people feel, and are both aware of and concerned about. When program development takes the time to test the reality of the need, there is better assurance that the process will be a success....

The Norwich Community study and the Virginia Water Project grew out of needs identified by the people themselves.... The Women's Center program grew out of a professional awareness of the problems of battered women; the Stop Gap Program emerged from professional assessment of the critical employment needs of ex-offenders.

After a need is perceived, institutional commitments to meet it must be solicited and secured. "The simple fact is that most all community solutions necessitate broad community support." Existing organizations must be brought together to help alleviate existing problems.

Once community support for a program has been generated, a program model has to be formed and approved. "A model may have a great deal of sex appeal but may, in fact, not be related to the need which has been identified.... Almost as important is the reality or achievability of the model. Is it realistic? Is it achievable? Thus, the model idea should be translated into specific goals and objectives that can be measured and evaluated."

The solution must then be presented and packaged in a way that will encourage people to contribute their energy toward its implementation. "A program model may have to be altered in some form to get the support necessary to make it fly." Once support is generated, it must be cemented into a permanent base for the program. In this way, the program is institutionalized and made a permanent part of the service structure for the community.

This has been the history of many TAP programs: they are designed in response to a need perceived either by the poor themselves or by social outreach workers, are funded and implemented by TAP, and are then institutionalized by being passed on to other organizations or set up independently.

TAP has taken dozens of programs through this procedure. Some have fallen down at one or another of the steps involved, but the best have flourished. The following pages provide some glimpses of program life.

Social Service Programs

Senior Citizens Organization for Opportunity Program (SCOOP). One of the most forgotten segments of the population is the elderly poor. A large proportion of old people

55

are poor because they have to live on fixed incomes eaten away by inflation or because they have inadequate financial resources to meet their expenses, which are often higher than average because of greater medical care needs.

TAP began a dozen senior citizens' groups throughout the Fifth Planning District. These groups, working autonomously within their communities, made changes in the way food was distributed to the elderly and arranged discounts at local pharmacies. Since transportation is often a problem for the elderly, particularly those living in outlying or rural areas, a transportation pool was organized to take seniors to hospitals, clinics, the commodity distribution center, and to social functions at the senior citizens' centers.

Loneliness and isolation are problems that plague the elderly. TAP organized a systematic program for senior citizens to call each other, both for company and as a safety check.

Homemaker Service. The Homemaker Service program was initiated to assist families in times of health or financial crisis, when parents were ill, or when a family member was incapacitated. Homemaker aides gave temporary help to stricken families, preparing meals, caring for children, arranging for health practitioner visits, and, above all, simply showing that the community was willing to step in and help when it was needed. The Homemaker Service program was administered through Family Service-Traveler's Aid and sent nine trained field workers out into the TAP service area.

Legal Aid. The poor, particularly those who are uneducated, are prey to a variety of contract manipulations of hire-purchase schemes. Some TAP area residents had signed contracts to buy property under the impression that the document was a lease. Others bought used appliances under the impression that the appliances were new. Still others have warranty problems, child support problems, marital separation problems, and the usual broad spectrum of legal ills.

TAP acquired funding to start the Legal Aid Society of the Roanoke Valley. Legal Aid, which worked in close contact with and at the pleasure of the Virginia State Bar, accepted only clients who were unable to pay a standard fee and only cases where no fee would be forthcoming (damages suits were not accepted).

Legal Aid has worked with clients and the courts to get the most satisfactory resolution to problems. Legal Aid's primary role has been to keep low-income families from going deeper into poverty or from losing lawful rights simply because they cannot afford a lawyer's fee.

In addition, the Legal Aid Society works to see where laws ought to be changed and tries to change them, either through legal arguments or by proposing new laws.

Food Programs. It remains a continuing irony in the United States that large quantities of edible food get discarded by food producers while, often in the same area, the poor go hungry.

TAP began to take advantage of this surplus of unmarketable food by starting the Foodbank. It took months of cooperation with federal agencies, food industry groups, local organizations, and local government welfare agencies to get the Foodbank started. But a way was worked out to gather and distribute the thousands of tons of dented cans, broken boxes, outdated produce, and production overruns that the food industry had been discarding as a matter of course.

The Foodbank start-up team included representatives from TAP and state and local governments. The Southwest Virginia Community Development Fund youth project renovated the Foodbank warehouse as a training project for their building trades classes. The students completed the job for $3,500—the cost of supplies. Once the warehouse and distribution mechanisms were in place, the Foodbank began distributing surplus food to the needy.

The Foodbank is supported by massive donations from the food industry, producers, distributors, and wholesalers. The Foodbank goods are then distributed to member agencies and local groups, who hand them out at no charge to the recipients.

In the face of federal budget cuts for food programs, coupled with increased demand, the Foodbank has helped member agencies, such as the Salvation Army, keep up their food distribution programs at an optimal level.

Much of the Foodbank's stock is supplied through the Second Harvest Foodbank Network, a national coalition of similar programs that collects surplus food from major industry producers. But TAP continues working to make the Roanoke Valley food industry aware of the program by emphasizing the need for local donations.

Concern for helping disadvantaged families get more nutritious meals prompted TAP to take an active part in dietary and food program reforms. The "Save-a-Buck" cooperative was started as a food-shopping club. Residents in the neighborhood banded together to buy staple items in bulk, thereby avoiding the usual retail markup. Other food-buying clubs were started in TAP's service area, but eventually administrative problems caused them to disband.

Such direct solutions still did not attack the root problems experienced by TAP clients. So TAP began individual client nutrition counseling, nutrition information workshops, summer feeding programs for children, and community truck garden programs. TAP also helped families qualify for and obtain food stamps, WIC (Women, Infants, and Children) supplements, and other federally funded or distributed food. During the federal government's surplus cheese programs, TAP organized and conducted cheese giveaways in the Roanoke area.

"Our Hope" Credit Union. Many poor individuals do not trust banks or large financial institutions. As a consequence, they cannot get credit to make large purchases or home repairs or must pay usurious interest rates to retailers.

The "Our Hope" credit union was chartered with federal funds and encouraged low-income people to make deposits and take out loans. The credit union's goal was to make loans available at reasonable cost to those who otherwise would be unable to get them and to encourage sound financial management by its members. In many cases, poor families use their money unwisely, and TAP attempted to assist the poor in making the most of their limited funds.

Alcohol and Drug Abuse Programs. Economic deprivation leads to social and emotional deprivation. Poverty exacerbates despair, hopelessness, and passivity. A poor person may find it easier to buy a bottle of wine than to confront personal problems. It is often cheaper to drink than to consult a marriage counselor or psychiatrist. And for teenagers, drugs are accessible, profitable, and attractive. TAP's activities in the social service field have included alcohol and drug abuse programs.

Alcoholism tends to perpetuate poverty. Alcoholics are often caught in an endless cycle of liquor, social, and legal problems. The TAP Alcohol Services program is designed to meet the needs of the low-income alcoholic and his family. It provides alcohol education and pre-crisis intervention.

TAP's first alcohol program grant from the Office of Economic Opportunity (OEO) in 1971 paved the way for an alcohol-counseling center in downtown Roanoke. TAP then served as a grantee from the National Institute for Alcohol and Alcohol Abuse for a program that included mental health services and a detoxification center/alcohol-counseling facility on Shenandoah Avenue, in a building donated to TAP by Evans Products.

The noncriminal nature of alchoholism is widely recognized, yet alcoholics continue to be processed through the criminal justice system. When a chronic alcoholic is arrested repeatedly and acquires a long criminal record, he is being punished for what is fundamentally an illness.

In cooperation with the Municipal Court of Roanoke, Alcoholics Anonymous, and local government, TAP began HELP, Inc. This separate organization runs a halfway house for male alcoholics in the Roanoke Valley. HELP's facilities are available to those charged with being drunk in public and enables them to return to their jobs and families without going to jail.

The house offers rehabilitation and job counseling. Halfway house personnel work closely with the local courts, which refer potential clients. The facility accommodates 28 men at a time; at the inception of the program, TAP provided for a cook and a counselor on duty 24 hours a day, seven days a week. HELP, Inc. has been successfully spun off to the United Fund and is now completely independent and self-supporting.

A similar facility to HELP's halfway house is Bethany Hall, a temporary shelter for women alcoholics. TAP is assisting Bethany Hall with fundraising and gives technical assistance to the shelter.

Family Planning. Family size is statistically linked to poverty. The larger a family, the greater the chances are that it will be poor. Poor families are often burdened by unwanted, neglected children, who grow into hostile, uncaring adults. They have children of their own and thus perpetuate the poverty cycle.

TAP initiated family-planning services in the Roanoke Valley in 1968. The family-planning effort included outreach to poor neighborhoods and operation of a clinic where birth control information could be obtained. TAP funded a family-planning specialist and continued to run the program until 1971, when the family-planning functions were transferred to the local chapter of Planned Parenthood.

Recreation Programs. Recreation programs provide a useful outlet for youthful energy, a directed avenue of interaction for young people, and a way of using leisure time for cooperative activities. Recreation can also be considered a form of training. By playing together, teenagers and children can learn social skills and cooperative work habits.

Poor neighborhoods, however, rarely provide recreational facilities or organized programs. When neighborhoods lack facilities and recreation workers, young people can get into trouble simply out of boredom.

One of TAP's most important contributions to Roanoke's recreational facilities was the swimming pool construction program. In 1967, TAP began planning for construction of swimming pools in poor neighborhoods. Eventually, four small pools were completed on Roanoke city property. The venture was a cooperative one between the city of Roanoke and TAP; TAP paid to construct the pools while the city made the land available.

For the first few years, TAP maintained and staffed the pools. After the fourth year, however, the pools were turned over to the Roanoke city government as a permanent addition to the city's recreation program. Through the TAP swimming pools, many inner-city youngsters were able to participate for the first time in swimming classes and water sports.

In the northeast area of Roanoke, TAP organized a youth council to focus on teenagers' needs. As a result, a teen lounge was started in a cinderblock building overlooking Washington Park.

Community Organization

The poor are often politically powerless. They have a low

voting percentage, have little input into the government, and do not participate in local and community activities. In many cases, all that is needed to improve the poor's participation in community government is to help them help themselves.

TAP's Community Organization program has mobilized the poor by helping them form independent organizations around issues that are of paramount concern to them. Staff workers go out to the neighborhoods, working with large and small groups of residents to provide youth recreation, to identify community problems, and to increase support for existing or proposed programs. The goal is to help local groups bring about social change that will benefit the poor.

Community organizers help the poor to isolate key areas of need, such as housing, welfare, health services, recreation, education, drug abuse, and youth employment. In addition, groups have been formed to promote community safety. Community organizers conduct surveys of residents, program users, or other target groups to find ways in which services can be improved.

In the case of immediate physical needs, Community Organization has worked to help the poor with problems of housing code enforcement and urban renewal. The community organizers also worked with neighborhood groups, school systems, the police department, and planning groups, such as the Fifth Planning District and the Roanoke Valley Council of Community Services, to bring increased safety to citizens of the TAP service area. A youth-police lab was formed, which helped foster better relations between young people and the police of the Roanoke Valley.

Community outreach workers also help poor people in crisis find the proper agency to help them. As organizers canvass the target areas, they spread the word about TAP and government services to neighborhood residents. The organizers continually make referrals to all of TAP's component agencies and other public and private programs. While delivery of services to those needing them is often fragmentary, this kind of referral outreach can help correct scatter-shot ways of applying social assistance and remove duplication. In addition, Community Organization workers help youths and the disaffected overcome alienation and difficulties connected with school integration, political conflicts, and other problems.

The Community Organization component of TAP has enabled the poor people in the Roanoke Valley to have a voice in their community. TAP has encouraged the poor to speak up about their concerns. The TAP community organizers have helped ease racial tensions, promote better public transportation systems, support drug rehabilitation groups, and solve neighborhood problems.

Jobs and Economic Development

America has always styled itself the land of opportunity, and for many years, this country did provide land and work for anyone with the initiative to get it. To the west, open country stretched to the horizon, ripe for development; in California, gold filtered down the streams. There was always a new frontier to settle, always work to be done.

But the social pressures and prejudices that kept the classes apart in the old world were still at work in the new. Slaves were given their nominal freedom, but most had no property, no skills, and nowhere to go. They remained on their farms as poor sharecroppers; many migrated to major urban areas in search of work. Sometimes it was available; sometimes it was not.

Many problems of employment are also problems of color. Growing up in segregated neighborhoods, attending segregated schools, and participating in segregated activities meant that most blacks were raised to be nonparticipants in society. Although only 20 percent of the poor in Roanoke are black, half of the blacks in the valley are poor. A large percentage of black households are headed by women; black

63

women are the most likely to be unemployed, and when actually working, they earn less than half of what a white man earns.

Unemployment also hits the uneducated. The workers least likely to be hired are those who did not complete high school. And in today's age of technological advancement, there is less and less unskilled work to be performed. The new jobs being created by industry call for education and skills, skills the poor simply do not have. As the world changes and advances, these people are left farther and farther behind.

Even if a poor person wants to work, he or she may be unemployable. Unskilled, inexperienced, and uneducated poor people do not usually have jobs; in fact, they may never have held a steady job and may be incapable of finding or keeping a job. They may have unrealistic attitudes about what they can hope to accomplish, or they may be ignorant of the opportunities available. In any case, there is a hard layer of poverty unemployment at the bottom of the economy—unemployment that may not be reflected in the job search figures because the poorest men and women have stopped searching.

The cycle of poverty self-perpetuates. Lacking money, the poor suffer from physical and intellectual deprivation. They tend to drop out of school without acquiring the skills or incentives to find a job. Unable to produce useful work, they have no money, and their children are forced to live the whole cycle out once again.

TAP believes that every capable adult must have a job. The New Deal had attempted to solve the joblessness problem institutionally; when the jobs were created, unemployed workers rose to fill them. TAP recognized that, in its client groups, the unemployed could not even get jobs that were available because they were unqualified. Institutionalization of job creation is not a viable solution to the problems of most unemployed poor people. While a new building project creates jobs for carpenters, it does nothing to help a man without training or skills.

The Community Action program has worked to help the unemployed on an individual basis. Although jobs were created, they were transitional, enabling someone without education or experience to acquire both and equip himself for jobs available in the ordinary market. The focus has been on the person, not the job.

Under the initial community action grant, TAP took a look at the different causes of unemployment and underemployment among the poor. It tried to isolate each component of the problem, to focus on a group that suffered from that type of problem, and to train or reeducate the members of the group to be productive workers.

Until the adoption of the Comprehensive Employment and Training Act (CETA), TAP's manpower efforts were concentrated into three main programs. Each was directed at a separate segment of the poor population, but each was designed to graduate a self-sufficient, employable worker into the normal employment environment.

Neighborhood Youth Corps. The Neighborhood Youth Corps (NYC) program was funded for TAP by the U.S. Department of Labor. The goal of the corps was to provide paid work experience for young people between 16 and 22 whose families' incomes were below the poverty line. NYC enrollees were given work experience, income, and encouragement to return to school or stay in school. The three subdivisions of the program—Out of School, In School, and Summer Youth Corps—addressed dropouts, potential dropouts, and students on their summer break who were in danger of staying out of school.

Before beginning a work program, NYC participants were given aptitude tests, health examinations, and guidance in selecting a field of work. During the period of employment, the enrollees attended unpaid counseling sessions to discuss problems with their jobs or personal lives. If trouble developed, participants were able to change fields or jobs within the program.

The out-of-school program enrollees worked for 32 hours per week while attending 6 hours of remedial education classes and 2 hours of personal and vocational counseling. Out-of-school participants worked for county governments, the Roanoke City Department of Parks, the Virginia Society for Crippled Children, and other areas where helping hands were needed. They were usually placed in aide positions, assisting an experienced worker in a given career field. In theory, observation of a career professional would encourage the participants to return to school, further their own education, and possibly become professional workers themselves.

The in-school NYC program assigned 10 hours of work each week to students who were currently in high school. These students could choose from 21 different job classifications in nonprofit agencies in TAP's service area. For many students, the money earned at their part-time jobs enabled them to buy necessary supplies for high school and thus served to keep them in school.

During the summer, work opportunities were offered in 32 different job classifications. Each Summer Youth Corps participant received 10 weeks of paid work, up to 25 hours per week, and an hour of counseling per week.

NYC graduates emerged with training in vocational subjects such as barbering, welding, auto mechanics, cosmetology, retail sales, nursing aide training, secretarial science, computer keypunching, upholstering, and laboratory technology. They learned good work habits, and many came to appreciate the sense of accomplishment and self-worth that hard work brings.

The in-school and Summer Youth Corps programs were successful at encouraging participants to continue in school. For both programs, the dropout rate was approximately 1 percent; 99 percent of the youth corps participants who were still in school or between grades either graduated or returned to school. The out-of-school program, while the source of advancement for many participants, was less successful overall. Approximately one-half of the out-of-school participants moved on to other jobs or returned to school.

Operation Mainstream. Operation Mainstream employed older workers, those over 40, who had poor work histories and few skills. To be eligible, an enrollee had to be chronically unemployed, with poor prospects for the future, and unable to secure assistance or training through other federal programs.

Operation Mainstream was designed to give paid work experience that helped maintain and improve public lands. Activities for these older workers included managing and developing natural resources in federal, state, and local parks. For one day each week, and during periods of inclement weather, participants took part in remedial education classes.

The TAP Operation Mainstream participants worked in the George Washington and Thomas Jefferson national forests. They built campsites, nature trails, and recreational areas, as well as helping foresters in conservation and timber management.

New Careers. TAP's New Careers program sought to place disadvantaged adults, particularly those who lacked traditional education or work experience, in paraprofessional positions. There are many technical and professional job duties that do not require the full expertise of a trained employee. Teachers and librarians, for example, often can use assistance in handling their routine job duties.

Throughout the New Careers program, the Department of Labor provided funding to TAP to subsidize wages of trainees in subprofessional positions. The program aimed to give trainees sufficient job skills to become permanent, unsubsidized employees of their sponsoring agencies.

TAP New Careers trainees were placed in nonprofit or public agencies in the Roanoke Valley area. They served as teacher aides, laboratory assistants, and nurses aides, among others. Enrollees were able to see professionals at work, participate in professional activities, and learn about the field they had chosen. Many went on to become teachers, librarians, or other professionals.

In the first year of the program, New Careers employees spent 40 hours a week in training, 30 hours at their jobs, 2 hours in counseling, 6 hours in remedial education classes, and 2 hours in unstructured study. In the second year, the workload remained at 30 hours, with 9 hours of vocational training and 1 hour of counseling. Courses available to New Careers trainees included English, psychology, sociology, and a variety of other classes at Virginia Western Community College.

TAP's role in these three programs went far beyond merely administering the funds and arranging for the trainees. TAP outreach personnel worked closely with employers, encouraging them to participate in training sessions and to hire manpower program trainees. TAP itself hired New Careers trainees, placing them in recreation, outreach, and administrative positions. TAP provided its employees training in the public service field, enabling them to find jobs with local governmental agencies or other public service agencies in the community.

CETA. In 1974, the increasing bureaucratic burden of the manpower training programs, coupled with a collapsing job market, led to the enactment of the Comprehensive Employment and Training Act (CETA). CETA abolished previous categorical programs and created a new act for administration by the Department of Labor. The CETA funds were uncategorized, giving local jurisdictions more discretion in their use. Under the OEO programs, funds had been earmarked for specific uses, such as programs for youths or migrant workers. This led to inflexibility in program planning; a city faced with the closing of a major manufacturing plant, for example, was unable to use its youth-training funds for industrial worker reeducation.

Under CETA, funds were administered by a separate office in the local government. Every urban area with more than 100,000 population was provided with a CETA office and funding. Grants were to be used primarily for direct training and wages, and limits were set on the amount that could be spent for administrative costs.

TAP's employment programs became subcontracts administered by the Roanoke CETA office. TAP operated Outreach, Work Experience, and Counseling programs, in addition to youth employment programs. CETA employees also were placed in TAP to perform outreach for other services.

The CETA Work Experience program gave a new beginning to its participants, providing meaningful jobs with public and private nonprofit organizations. The enrollees were frequently single parents and heads of households, and often, they were black women. The program gave them a chance to build up their working backgrounds in an unpressured atmosphere, with the opportunity to go on from a simple position to a more complex, well-paying one.

Enrollees for the Work Experience program were selected because they had some marketable skill, such as typing. They developed their already present skills while they gained confidence on the job and learned good work habits. This enabled many of them to enter advanced training positions and permanent jobs.

Most Work Experience positions were more than menial and have led to higher-than-minimum-wage jobs. The 75 percent positive termination rate for the program demonstrated its effectiveness in creating useful, employable, upwardly mobile workers.

Work Experience also benefited TAP directly. Because enrollees were paid from congressional funds, TAP was able to hire untrained workers, give them experience, and eventually take them on as permanent, TAP-paid employees.

In 1975, TAP geared up to take advantage of the new Public Service Employment program (PSE), which gave temporary jobs to the unemployed. TAP placed people in slots on short notice, 36 the first year. In 1977, the PSE program grew rapidly as the recession deepened. TAP mobilized to develop new jobs within the agency and PSE Special Projects to serve the many needs of Roanoke's poor. The 121 new positions allowed an expansion in delivery of services to rural areas.

The weatherization program (which will be discussed later) had always depended on CETA workers, but with the new PSE workers, the program was expanded. In addition, Black Lung Outreach, Parks Development, Food-Buying Clubs, Health Assessment and Prevention Education, Alleghany County Court Project, Rural Youth Activities, and the Jefferson National Forest Project were staffed entirely by CETA workers. On-the-job training and salaries benefited hundreds of workers in the Roanoke Valley, who, in turn, contributed needed services to the community.

TAP CETA workers also operated a Scholarship Clearinghouse, a one-year project that helped 161 low-income students apply to college or for vocational training. The staff also tutored G.E.D. (graduate equivalency diploma) candidates and helped high-school juniors get fee waivers so they could take the Scholastic Aptitude Tests.

CETA was abolished by the federal government early in the Reagan administration, and current CETA-dependent programs at TAP are being phased out. CETA acquired a dubious reputation because some contractors misused CETA funds. CETA employers were caught hiring unqualified participants, using CETA workers in unsuitable jobs, and laying off CETA workers as soon as their government funds were exhausted. The program will be replaced with a different jobs package, but as of this writing, it has not been established.

What of TAP's contributions to the problems of the unemployed? In order to judge, one must consider the two kinds of unemployment. The first is economic, or the normal ebb and flow of jobs according to the current industrial climate. The second is cultural, and it affects generations of potential workers who do not have the skills, training, inclination, motivation, or opportunity to get jobs.

An automobile plant worker who has been laid off is in the first category and is likely to find work when times improve. A high-school dropout who cannot read is in the second category and will continue to be unemployed no matter what jobs may be available.

TAP's programs attempted to help those poor who would not have been able to get jobs through normal means. TAP's goals were to provide training, education, and jobs.

Many of those who benefited from TAP's programs got their start at TAP itself. TAP practiced what it preached, and many of its most successful employees started at the organization as trainees or program participants. Hundreds of staff members have "graduated" from TAP to other Roanoke Valley nonprofit or government agencies, while others have returned to school or gone on to college. Once given a chance, employees have moved "up and out," increasing the participation of minorities and the underprivileged in social service organizations.

But the problem of cultural unemployment remains, as large and seemingly insoluble as ever. TAP programs such as Head Start and family planning, approach families and children to equip them for the American labor market. But for those adults with no work history, no education, and no skills, the picture continues to look bleak. The labor market grows increasingly heavy with technical jobs that require ever-increasing amounts of skill. Employers are not willing to hire menial workers with little to offer, particularly in times of high unemployment, when skilled workers are readily available.

For those with no work history, TAP provided an opportunity to acquire experience. But for many of the non-participating poor, the barriers to getting and keeping a job go beyond the lack of opportunity. The concepts of promptness, reliability, and initiative are foreign to the culturally unemployed. TAP attacked some of these problems with counseling, classwork, and training in such peripheral employment skills as grooming and attitude.

TAP also encouraged employers in the Roanoke Valley to hire poor workers and give them a start. The first job is the most important, particularly for a person with no work history and few chances. For the poor who were victims of discrimination, this approach was useful.

Southwest Virginia Community Development Fund. In many cases, once a neighborhood declines into poverty, it tends to stay that way. Industry relocates out of the area or, if it remains, starts to falter. Jobs are eliminated. Improving the economic climate of an impoverished area betters the condition of its residents by bringing in people, money, and jobs.

The Southwest Virginia Community Development Fund was started by TAP as a nonprofit corporation to promote economic development of Roanoke's inner city and nearby pockets of rural poverty. TAP's staff participated in the organization and preparation of a grant proposal that led to funding of $547,543 from the Office of Economic Opportunity in 1969.

Opportunities Industrialization Center. Uneducated or untrained workers cannot compete in today's technically oriented job market. Many older workers, those who had dropped out of high school years ago or had never learned a reasonable trade, are chronically unemployed or employed at salaries too low to support themselves and their families.

The Opportunities Industrialization Center (OIC), a TAP spin-off, has sought to retain unemployed or underemployed men and women so they could find jobs. In addition, OIC has recruited participants for basic education classes in such subjects as English, mathematics, history, economics, and business procedures. OIC workers are trained to qualify for new jobs offering better pay.

Areas of training have been geared to recognized labor shortages in the Roanoke Valley area. Workers have been given intensive instruction in such marketable skills as secretarial work, carpentry, plumbing, painting, sheet metal work, brick laying, auto mechanics, paper hanging, and roofing. Each OIC participant received individual counseling and, on completion of the program, help finding a job.

Special Programs

TAP's fresh approach to problem solving has led it down some unusual paths in its attempts to help the poor.

Transportation, for example, is a severe problem for the elderly, for the poor who live out of range of public transportation, and for the disabled. Services and programs often go unused by those qualified for them simply because they cannot make it into the office for screening or application. TAP solved the access problem with Roanoke Area Dial-a-Ride (RADAR), which made transportation available to those who needed it.

Another problem for the poor is housing, which is often substandard and can be structurally or electrically unsafe. TAP's fire prevention program reached hundreds of homes, bringing information about fire prevention and smoke detectors.

TAP faced an unexpected problem after the fall of Vietnam, when hundreds of refugees flooded into the TAP service area. TAP immediately responded by organizing a Vietnamese service project. TAP staffers tutored refugee children in English and helped their parents find jobs and housing. A one-year grant resulted in publication of a Vietnamese newsletter that brought the refugees information about their new community.

TAP's community gardens program gave out seeds, gardening advice and assistance, and information. Many poor families could save money on food bills, increase their self-reliance, and derive satisfaction and accomplishment through gardening. TAP encouraged the formation of communal plots and home gardens.

Crisis relief was another problem that required a special approach. When a crisis strikes a poor family, the normal channels of assistance often move too slowly. Several days or weeks may go by while the welfare system adjusts to a family's suddenly changed circumstances. In such cases, TAP's emergency aid program helps out with food, fuel, rent money, and utility bills, on a one-time basis. TAP's emergency aid helped distribute the congressionally mandated fuel fund during the extremely cold winter of 1977.

As the variety of programs available in the Roanoke Valley multiplied, the need for a directory became clear. After all, what good are social welfare programs if the poor don't know about them? So TAP published *Where to Find Help*, a book listing all public assistance and community services in the valley, covering everything from family planning to welfare to housing to employment.

Beyond the Traditional

Many of the TAP programs discussed in this chapter could be considered traditional modes for attacking poverty. The programs have sought (1) to sustain a decent, if minimum, standard of living for people who generate insufficient income to maintain such a standard unassisted and (2) to prepare people to hold jobs that will generate sufficient income for a satisfactory life style.

There are several areas where TAP has gone beyond the traditional. It has used a "total home" approach to address the problems faced by women and children and to teach people how to live in houses as well as how to get them. It has treated the ex-offender population as the "forgotten poverty population" of the age. It has used a networking approach in dealing with a "hardware" problem of the poor—water and sanitation. These programs may well be TAP's greatest accomplishments. The following three chapters look at each of these in detail.

4

Making a House
A Home

*I've been there. I've been poor—dirt poor—and I'll never
forget what it was like. TAP has done a lot more for me
than pay me a salary. It's given me a chance to help some
people who really need it. You just wouldn't believe how
happy these people are to move into their own home.*

Betty Desper, to Mike Ives, September 1972

Although Betty Desper was born into a well-to-do family,
she faced the bleakest of poverty when she was 46 years old.
Her husband suffered a mental and physical breakdown
while working on a job—he was an electrician—in Blacksburg, Virginia. She had a child to feed, a house to pay for,
no money ("down to five potatoes ont time"), and no job
skills.

But Betty Desper is a survivor. To survive in the early
1960s, she walked three miles each way to a 14-hour-a-day
waitress job. Later, through an old school friend, she got
a job with TAP as a community organizer in Salem. It was
the lowest job at TAP, but with Bristow Hardin pushing
and bullying her every step of the way, Betty began to take
courses and to learn on the job. She organized people around
welfare rights, led pickets at Sears, and did other outreach
work. By the time she talked to Mike Ives of the *Roanoke
Times & World News* in September 1972, she was heading

TAP's housing department. Ives reported the visit in his "My Turn" column:

Betty Desper is a large, formidable looking woman who bustles around giving houses to poor people.

Actually, she doesn't give 'em away, but she knows more ways to get housing loans for poor people than anybody else I can think of with the possible exception of Robin Hood, who is retired.

Betty started out six years ago as a neighborhood worker for TAP (Total Action Against Poverty). Her original "neighborhood" was the Cat Hill area of Roanoke County, which is a pretty good place to fight poverty, since there's a lot of it up there.

"When I first went there I found that the problem everybody was complaining about was housing," Betty recalls. "I found one family living in refrigerator boxes. They needed houses but they didn't have any money for a down payment."

So what Betty did was nose around various programs trying to figure out a way to get houses for these people. That's how she stumbled onto FHA (Farmer's Home Administration)[abbreviated in text as FmHA].

Although it was a pretty well kept secret, Betty found out that FHA had a stack of money that it was willing to loan to poor people to buy houses. Armed with this knowledge, Betty bustled around here and there, getting people to fill out applications and transporting them to sign papers. Before you knew it, a lot of poor people were moving into houses with indoor johns and other unheard of luxuries.

Needless to say, Betty gets a large kick out of getting houses for these people. One of her greatest triumphs was a case involving two old maids in their 80's who needed a home. "We got 'em a 33 year loan," Betty cackles delightedly. That's what kind of a saleman she is.

After awhile, the people over at TAP began noticing that Betty was getting an awful lot of houses for an awful lot of poor people, so they decided to set up a rural housing staff. They also decided to make Betty head of it, since she seemed to be slicker than somewhat at prying money out of FHA.

At present, Betty has a staff of five whom she alternately bullies and cajoles into getting out in the field and signing up more people for more houses. It's become sort of a passion with her. She has this dream of seeing every family in the rural areas of Rockbridge, Botetourt, Craig and Roanoke counties owning their own homes.

Her husband is beginning to think that she doesn't know when to quit. Betty went on vacation to Indiana a few weeks ago to look up some relatives out near Terre Haute. While she was there she discovered that her great-great-grandfather was an Indian, a fact that intrigues her.

She also discovered that nobody in Terre Haute had ever heard of FHA, so before she left she had signed up six poor families for home loans, and had talked her cousin into stumping the countryside looking for more people who could qualify for loans.

The FHA plan, Betty hastens to add, isn't just some pie-in-the-sky experiment. She points out that of the 90 people her staff has helped to get loans through FHA, only one has suffered foreclosure, which is a pretty strong batting average.

And there's more to come. "The word is out," Betty says happily. "We're presently working with over 500 families, and we're getting more calls everyday." She waves a fistful of loan applications in one hand and says cheerfully, "Just keep those cards and letters rollin' in, folks. We can handle 'em somehow."

TAP has probably done a lot more for Betty Desper than pay her salary. But when you think about it, she's done a helluva lot more for TAP than punch a time clock.

Housing the Poor

One of the most important goals for the middle class in America is owning and maintaining a nice place to live. Home ownership is taken for granted, as is the presence of plumbing, heating, washing, and cooking facilities. While many families will do without a dishwasher, for example, they could not even imagine living without a sink.

Not so for poor families, for whom housing is never accepted without worry. Actual ownership, for most, is out of the question, and many cannot even handle the concept. A poor household is likely to be overcrowded, underheated, in bad repair, and generally owned by someone else—a landlord, a slumlord, or, in the case of a housing project, the government. Poor dwellings frequently do not meet the housing code standards set by the government; once the overall tone of a poor neighborhood is established, the tendency is for landlords to allow already shabby housing to deteriorate further because "only poor people live there."

Poor neighborhoods also are deficient in normal city services. Since the poor do not pay as much in taxes, and since they are, in many cases, members of minority groups, trash collection, street lighting, and police patrols are given low priority by city governments. The poor are also voiceless; they then not to complain, and they do not vote.

TAP's efforts to improve the housing situation of the Roanoke Valley have been broad-based and directed in several areas. One way housing has been improved, indirectly, is through the Community Outreach program. Outreach workers have encouraged the formation of community committees and neighborhood groups; spokespeople from these groups have gone to city hall to discuss housing code violations with city inspectors. In this sense, some housing problems are ameliorated merely by organizing the poor and giving them a chance at representation in the government.

In the direct fight for housing, however, TAP has operated programs in three major areas: weatherization, housing rehabilitation, and housing counseling. In addition, TAP has built low-income housing, rehabilitated donated houses for sale, and been instrumental in planning for low-income housing projects in the Roanoke Valley.

Weatherization. "Weatherizing" houses is a simple enough process, and one, again, that the middle class takes for granted. A homeowner faced with heat loss will put up storm windows, insulate the roof, and plug cracks in the walls. An impoverished renter may not have the knowledge, and certainly does not have the funds, to take steps to conserve energy and prevent heat loss. For the elderly, drafty and badly insulated houses are a special health hazard. And for the rural poor, a badly insulated house can mean excessive amounts of time spent gathering wood or a disproportionate amount of the family income spent on heating; the choice between eating and keeping warm is not one any family should have to make.

TAP's first weatherization project started in 1974 with a small grant from the Cave Spring Jaycees. The money was used to purchase transparent plastic sheeting and lumber, which were used to manufacture makeshift storm windows for poor homes. The Department of Energy contributed additional funds, and a full-scale program of insulating, roofing, and repairing houses was begun.

Weatherization service is provided free of charge to poverty-level homeowners. With the aid of CETA funds to pay workers, the weatherization crews install storm windows, blow in insulation, caulk cracks, and make minor home repairs. This work is especially important to the elderly, who do not have the strength to make repairs themselves and who are greatly susceptible to weather-related illness.

In addition to helping homeowners, weatherization programs also have given hundreds of unemployed and underemployed workers training in housing trades. After working with weatherization teams, workers are well equipped to get jobs in construction or home improvements.

Housing Rehabilitation. In 1975, TAP put together a Comprehensive Neighborhood Improvement Plan for the area near its headquarters in Roanoke. The plan included interviews with homeowners in the target area to assess what they felt were their primary needs. A large percentage of the residents cited home improvements as the primary concern; most of the work involved electrical wiring, plumbing, and structural repairs.

The Comprehensive Neighborhood Improvement Project, which implemented the plan, was designed as a "self-help" housing rehabilitation effort for the poorest people, who live in the worst housing. The project sought to correct the most critical safety and sanitary deficiencies of their houses in accordance with the housing code. The object of self-help is to make families realize that housing rehabilitation, or any improvement in their lives, depends on them. With this program, low-income families can begin to learn what self-help means and to cultivate pride for what can be accomplished.

In order to qualify for help, the family must become financially involved in the rehabilitation (at whatever scale possible) and must share (in whatever way practical) in the actual physical work.

The Housing Rehabilitation program did more than rehabilitate houses: it helped invigorate the lives of low-income residents; it trained the previously unemployed and uneducated in construction skills; and it enlarged the community's understanding of housing problems. Poor people began to see the self-help housing rehabilitation approach as an efficient solution to a number of common problems.

Under contract with the City of Roanoke Redevelopment Housing Authority, TAP rehabilitated 12 houses in the first year of the program and has progressed since then to improve approximately 8 to 12 houses per year.

Under TAP's Housing Rehabilitation program, workers were paid with CETA funds. The city of Roanoke, however, operated a program from the Department of Housing and Urban Development (HUD) that provided direct federal loans to finance rehabilitation in urban renewal and housing code enforcement areas certified by the housing authority. By financing rehabilitation to bring the property up to the applicable code requirements, the HUD loans prevented the unnecessary demolition of low-income housing and the further deterioration of basically sound and usable structures. This program was planned to supplement and support the TAP Housing Rehabilitation program in revitalizing city housing.

Housing Counseling. In addition to helping rehabilitate houses, TAP developed a program to assist owners with housing problems. The philosophy behind TAP's Housing Counseling service is that families with housing problems have multiple causes for those problems; the issue is not necessarily confined to housing. In 1975, a counseling program was developed to identify causes of housing crises and ways to help clients out of those crises. Each client's situation is unique; so each strategy must be individually designed. The counseling staff at one point consisted of five people, but in the wake of budget cuts and funding problems, it has dwindled to one. The staff has counseled families about such issues as default and delinquent mortgages, rental payments, emergency relocation, pre-occupancy rental, money management for rent and utilities, and energy conservation.

The TAP Housing Counseling component was recognized as a certified housing counseling agency in 1975 by the Department of Housing and Urban Development; the first HUD grant was received in 1977. That year, in addition, the Farmer's Home Administration asked TAP to provide information to families so they could realistically evaluate their financial ability for homeownership and to work with mortgage lenders to prevent defaults. In 1978, TAP helped reduce delinquencies in its area by up to 40 percent.

TAP's housing counselors screen prospective clients to avoid duplicating services provided by other agencies. And while TAP's counselors are primarily intended to serve low-income families, the HUD counselors are not restricted by the income of their clients. A family experiencing a housing crisis is eligible for help no matter what its income. Clients must sign a release of information form, because of the Privacy Act of 1974, before the counselor can deal with other agencies or individuals.

As the TAP housing counselors put it,

> We rarely decline to counsel. The degree of our services is sometimes dependent on client cooperation. We do not assume a client will not cooperate until that client repeatedly ignores our suggestions. Some people have chronic patterns that years of counseling have not changed. Other people cannot be effectively counseled because of severe and acute emotional problems, or acute alcoholic toxification. These last people are referred to the Mental Health Services, or to the Alcoholic Detoxification Center, which TAP operates in conjunction with the Mental Health Services.

> We discuss the problem with each client as he or she sees it. We believe the key to effective counseling is listening. After the client states his or her problem, we evaluate it and offer suggestions and a plan of action.

> Clients are terminated when any of these conditions prevail: (1) a temporary problem is totally resolved; (2) the client shows a total lack of cooperation; (3) the client disappears and cannot be located; (4) the client moves out of our service area. Clients are urged to recontact us. If 30 days have passed without recontact, we will phone, write, or visit the client to ascertain current status.

Counselors deal directly with clients, landlords, and creditors to try and prevent evictions and defaults. Where evictions occur, TAP counselors make arrangements for the moving and storage of possessions put out on the street. It is not uncommon for an evicted family to lose, not only its home, but also its furniture and clothing through theft after eviction. Where possible, counselors negotiate repayment programs for delinquent clients and teach budgeting.

83

In addition, counselors help families that are forced to move select a home, buy insurance, and manage and maintain their new home. Clients in need of housing are referred to realtors, landlords, and housing sources; whenever possible, TAP counselors attempt to place lower-income clients into HUD-subsidized units.

While clients come to TAP's housing counselors voluntarily, the Farmer's Home Administration (FmHA) regularly supplies TAP with a list of people with delinquent mortgages. TAP contacts those on the list and attempts through counseling to prevent foreclosures. FmHA estimates that each foreclosure costs them around $6,000; if TAP can prevent foreclosures, it is saving the government the costs of repossessing the home, as well as saving the home for its residents.

TAP was catapulted into the real estate business in 1968 when it received a donation of $241,000 worth of property. William P. Swartz, Jr., a Roanoke businessman and civic leader, donated 66 home sites and dwellings to TAP for use in helping the poor. Swartz said of his gift, "We hope that our contribution will stimulate others to look at the housing problem and take whatever action they can as private citizens to solve a delicate situation."

In order to cope with such an unprecedented and generous gift, TAP set up the Community Housing Corporation to administer and rehabilitate the donated properties. The corporation solicited funds from the Federal Housing Administration to finance improvements of existing units and construction of new homes on vacant lots. The existing houses were eventually rehabilitated and sold to low-income residents; on the vacant lots, new buildings were erected and sold to low-income families. The Community Housing Corporation has continued to build, refurbish, and rehabilitate houses.

In 1971, the corporation prepared an ambitious proposal to the Federal Housing Administration to build 176 housing units for the poor and elderly. The $3.5 million project was initially approved but later, after two years of negotiation, denied. TAP continues to sit on the board of the Community Housing Corporation and helped, in 1977, plan and develop a project to house the elderly. Other TAP housing activities included fighting for fair relocation payments to residents uprooted by the Kimball Renewal project in 1967, helping to start the Buena Vista Housing Development Corporation in 1969, and advocating a fair housing ordinance in Roanoke in 1972.

The need for decent housing remains a critical problem in the TAP service area. TAP's housing counselors refer clients to sources of public and low-cost housing, but such sources are in increasingly short supply. Weatherization and home improvement programs have made existing units safer, more energy efficient, and cleaner, but adequate housing availability remains a serious problem for the poor of the Roanoke Valley.

Uplifting the Women

The majority of people who live in poverty are women. If a woman is working, she earns less—approximately 59 percent less—than what a man earns. If she is retired, she collects a smaller pension—insurance companies maintain different pension scales for women. If she is married, she will probably outlive her husband by an average of 10 years, during which time she will have to support herself on a widow's pension. If she has children, they probably live with her, and she may be their only source of support.

Across the board, women have smaller incomes than men; this is true even of such professions as doctors and bank presidents. At the poverty level, a poor woman is probably poorer than a poor man. Half of poor families are headed by women, and a family headed by a woman has a greater chance of being poor. Women, with their smaller average salaries, start at a disadvantage; black women are victims of dual discrimination and are most likely to be poor.

Poor women, especially heads of households, are the homemakers and consumers. Consumer education programs for the poor are aimed almost entirely at women, who take care of the family's finances. If she is married, a poor woman who suffers abuse from her husband may not know where to turn for help; a single head of household may be too busy trying to make ends meet to be able to provide adequate child care.

When TAP began in 1965, women's problems were dealt with peripherally, through special programs like homemaker services, family planning, Head Start, and parent education. "Mothers' clubs" were formed to help working mothers care for their children. After 10 years, TAP recognized the need for a separate Women's Programs component, an arm of the organization designed to deal primarily with the multiple problems of poor women.

The Women's Center. Late in the summer of 1974, two women lawyers from Legal Aid approached TAP's planning staff to discuss the enormous number of clients they saw who had been victimized and beaten by their husbands. One solution they proposed was to develop and run a shelter for abused women and their children. TAP agreed to meet and discuss the problem and the proposed solution.

The first meeting included the Legal Aid attorneys, TAP staff, a private consultant, a representative from the National Organization for Women, and the supervisor of welfare for Roanoke city. A number of ideas were proposed, but at a second meeting a month later, the consensus of the group was that a women's shelter was needed. They also saw the need for a women's center to provide help for women in crisis who wanted counseling, information, and support.

The YWCA was eventually selected as the site for the women's center because of its proximity to downtown Roanoke and public transportation. The Women's Center opened in 1975 and was the first such center run by a community action agency. It remained at the YWCA until 1981, when it moved into the TAP building.

The women's shelter idea was adopted by the Brambleton Junior Women's Club, which formed Mahala, a private, nonprofit corporation, to seek funds for a shelter. After much persistence and hard work, the board of Mahala finally mangaged to rent a house in Roanoke with seven apartments. After volunteers spent three months cleaning, painting, and furnishing, Mahala admitted the first resident—a seventh-months-pregnant woman—in June 1980. TAP provides a residential manager, as well as screening and counseling for residents. Operating funds for the shelter come from private fundraising and the United Way.

In the Women's Shelter, Roanoke Valley women, who might otherwise be at the mercy of their families, have a place to go for refuge, as well as an understanding advocate. Since the renovation was completed, the shelter has remained full to capacity.

Women's Programs. Through the Women's Resources Center, TAP has conducted many programs aimed at the special needs of women. A Young Women's Project counseled pregnant teenagers in the Children's Home Society School, providing follow-up, counseling, support, and parenting education. Workshops and support groups started include the Forum on Women and Work, Legal Rights of Women, Assertiveness Training, Spouse Abuse, and Parents Support Group. The center also maintains a Rape Support Group and works closely with TAP Alcohol Services to help women affected by alcohol abuse.

In addition to their problems as women, many poor women face crises of education and consumer knowledge.

The average educational level for poor women is lower than for any other group; TAP's educational programs have made special efforts to help women who lack formal educational credentials earn a G.E.D. In the most successful cases, former welfare mothers have been able to finish high school, go on to college, and enter nursing and teaching professions as a result of encouragement from TAP staff.

Women as consumers have been aided by TAP's consumer education programs. Food shopping strategy workshops educated the poor about comparative pricing, unit pricing, and universal product codes. In addition, credit workshops helped women understand the true cost of credit and how to obtain it, if necessary.

TAP's programs, however, do not focus only on helping or information. The Women's Center conceived an idea for a celebration of women in the arts, and the "Artemis" festival was born. The first Artemis festival, in 1977, produced an elegant and engrossing book of poetry, art, short stories, and photography. The festival has since become an annual event, encouraging creative women to be proud of their talents and to continue to work with them. Artemis events include concerts, dance recitals, plays, art shows, poetry readings, and other forums for the display of women's arts.

TAP's Women's Programs took a giant step in recognizing the specific problems of poor women. Although programs previously had included women, there was no single place a woman could go and receive help. For a female head of household, for instance, the coordination between job search, child care, health maintenance, and housing is vital; yet until the women's component began, it was necessary to go from agency to agency to receive help in each of these areas. A job is useless to a poor mother if her child is left uncared for; TAP's counselors can work on several aspects of a woman's situation at the same time. TAP gives encouragement and placement assistance to women seeking nontraditional jobs; and for any poor woman who is insecure about her employability, this kind of support is essential.

Finally, TAP's women's component provides the backup that many women need. Often, women find it helpful to know that they are not alone in their problems; meetings and discussions with other women whose situation is similar can provide support to a distressed mother. The Women's Center at TAP provides program referral, job assistance, counseling, and, above all, hope for women who have no place else to go.

The women's component of TAP may someday be its most vital arm. A 1983 report by the U.S. Civil Rights Commission says that the "feminization-of-poverty" trend shows no sign of abating and predicts that minority families headed by women will dominate the poverty population by the year 2000. The rest of the poor, says the report, will be white women and children.

The report finds that:

- Between 1960 and 1981, the number of people in poor families headed by women increased 54 percent while the number dropped dramatically for male-headed households.
- The increasing trend of unwed mothers and divorce is the major contributor to poverty.
- Women with children, regardless of their previous economic circumstances, are usually poorer after their marriage ends. Of women awarded child support by a court, about a quarter never get a payment and another quarter get less than the full amount awarded.
- For poor women, access to child care often means the difference between self-support and welfare.
- The biggest factor in reducing women's poverty rate is welfare programs.
- Administration budget cuts may penalize the working poor and force some short-term welfare households into long-term dependency because some welfare recipients lose disposable income by working.

Saving the Children

Children are the saddest victims of poverty. A child born into a poor family has a 50-50 chance of growing up to be a poor adult and the parent of more poor children. Like a hereditary disease, poverty is passed down through generations, from parent to child in a seemingly endless cycle of deprivation. If unaided, a poor child will be poorly nourished, poorly educated, poorly adjusted, poorly socialized, poorly trained, and poorly adapted to live a productive adult life. Starting from before birth, a deprived child gets less of what children need, less of what more well-off children can take for granted, and less of the care that will ensure a good life.

Children are the most flexible link in the long chain of poverty. Childhood development studies have documented that crucial developmental stages are reached by the time a child is six. A child who comes from a home without books will have little incentive to read; a child whose parents do not play with him will be withdrawn. Much of a child's intellectual potential is formed by the time he begins school; yet during those years, deprived parents are unlikely to take any action to encourage the child's intellectual growth.

If a child receives inadequate educational training at home before he enters the first grade, he has a greater possibility of failing for the rest of his life.

Head Start. If a child is to escape from poverty, the best time to set new behavior patterns is in early childhood. When the Equal Opportunity Act of 1964 was passed, one of the key provisions allotted money for Head Start, a program to foster better early childhood development. Head Start gives preschool children from underprivileged backgrounds some of the enriching experience shared by their middle-class counterparts and prepares them for a challenging academic life.

90

The overall goal of Head Start programs is to bring about a greater degree of social competence in children and their families. Social competence means everyday effectiveness in dealing with the responsibilities in the present environment, be that school or, later, adult life. It is not just the child who benefits from Head Start—parent involvement is encouraged, and often an entire family will be helped by the placement of one child in a Head Start program. The Head Start program takes into account the relationship between intellectual growth, physical and mental health, nutrition, and the many other factors that influence and shape a child's development.

Head Start's goals, according to the manual, include improving the child's health; encouraging his ability to think, reason, and speak clearly; and developing a climate of confidence that makes him want to learn. Head Start also aims to help the child get along with his family, develop a reasonable attitude toward society, and acquire feelings of belonging to a community. The program offers the child a chance to see teachers, policemen, doctors, and other authority figures in an educational, nonthreatening situation, thereby promoting respect rather than fear. Overall, Head Start can help both the child and his family achieve a life of greater confidence, self-respect, and dignity.

The transition to school is difficult for a child, particularly for a child from a deprived background. Poor parents, like any other parents, raise children the way they themselves were raised, and this often does not give a child good preparation for school. Parents, particularly mothers of young children, often feel isolated, frustrated, and overwhelmed by their responsibilities. Their response to a constantly questioning child is to hush him up rather than to answer the questions on a level the child can understand. Small children are by nature noisy, energetic, disorderly, curious, and unpredictable; a mother may feel her child is hyperactive or abnormal when if fact he is simply doing the usual things for a child his age. A child may be seen as a burden and a nuisance rather than as an individual with special needs and interests.

Head Start begins the attack on the poverty cycle in the home. Parental involvement is a key part of the Head Start program. Parents of Head Start children can meet each other and discuss the different phases of childhood, the special needs of young children, and the ways in which children behave differently from adults. Head Start encourages parents to talk to others with the same concerns and problems.

Head Start teachers, as part of their duties, visit the children's homes to evaluate the family's situation. Parents are encouraged to serve as volunteers and to participate in various Head Start program committees.

The "academic" curriculum for Head Start is loosely organized and concentrates to a large extent on enrichment activities for the children. Field trips to farms, museums, and parks provide children with a glimpse of a world outside their own; many poor children have never been outside of their own neighborhoods. In addition, basic educational skills are stressed. Children work with colors, the alphabet, and numbers. Children are read to, a new experience for some of them. And they learn to play cooperatively with other children and to participate in group activities.

Children who appear retarded or who need special instruction are kept in the mainstream class but given extra attention by the teachers. Such individualized attention is possible because classes are small (no more than 15 children, usually). Each class is taught by a Head Start teacher, with 4 or more assistants, teacher aides, or volunteers also present. The average ratio is 1 teacher to 4 children, a situation that allows maximal personal attention for each child.

Another vital aspect of Head Start is nutrition. A child who is not well-fed cannot learn and cannot grow into a well-functioning adult. Some poor children face a lifetime of mental retardation because of malnutrition early in life. Although the Head Start program cannot totally compensate for a nutritionally poor diet at home, it does give the children meals that are, in some cases, nearly their complete diet. Head Start children are given a hot meal and a snack; a second meal is included if the child is at day care for long periods of time.

Head Start also provides health care and examinations to detect problems that might otherwise go untreated. There are many congenital or other health problems that can be corrected easily in childhood but cause serious damage later. Entering children are given eye, hearing, and medical examinations, and if necessary, glasses, orthopedic shoes, and other health aids are provided. Psychological counselors help students who have behavioral or psychological problems, conferring with parents as the need arises. Children are diagnosed early for conditions that can be cured while the child is young, and they receive medical care, including necessary inoculations, that can prevent a later disability.

Head Start was the first program of the war on poverty, and it was also the first program operated by TAP in the Roanoke Valley. Immediately after TAP was incorporated, a site was found for a Head Start center. The Loudon Head Start Center opened in 1965 for 105 preschoolers and 50 school-age children who needed afternoon care.

At the time when TAP's Head Start program got underway, there was no public kindergarten in the Roanoke Valley. Children were expected to start school when they reached age six, going directly into the first grade. Only those who attended private day-care centers had any experience in a classroom environment. This abrupt transition ensured adjustment problems for children from lower-income families.

After opening the first day-care center, TAP expanded its early childhood program to include 10 centers, in East

93

Roanoke, Lexington, Montvale, Fincastle, Glasglow, Salem, Loudon, Lincoln Terrace, Landstown, and at St. John's Church. Even at its maximum size, however, TAP's Head Start program was only able to reach around 20 percent of the eligible children in its service area.

During the difficult budgetary times of the 1970s, Head Start funds were one of the few areas that were not directly threatened. Funds were frozen and cut back, however, and budgetary problems forced the closing of three centers. Head Start continues to serve nearly 500 children in the Roanoke Valley, however.

While TAP frequently spun off its own programs to other local organizations, the Head Start program remained under TAP's control. One reason for this was the interrelationship between the Head Start program and other TAP programs; in many cases, participants in CETA or other job-training programs acquired experience working in TAP's day-care centers. In addition, Head Start is a politically popular program. Separating Head Start from TAP would probably deprive the agency of much-needed legislative support for its overall effort. Head Start is somewhat autonomous as a community action program, however. For example, Head Start teachers must be unionized separately from other TAP employees.

One of the major, though less direct, benefits accruing from TAP's Head Start program is greater job opportunities for adults. Many parents are given the freedom, through Head Start, to pursue full-time jobs. For this reason, not all of Head Start's children are from families below the poverty line; where Head Start can make a difference in a parent's employment prospects, the child is kept on.

Head Start also provides an opportunity for unemployed parents to volunteer at the centers. Many of the teacher aides are parents of Head Start children, and hundreds of volunteers have gone on to become salaried teachers. In a number of cases, women who started out as welfare mothers have ended up with college degrees in teaching, working as teachers and administrators in Head Start centers.

For parents who do have full-time jobs, TAP day-care centers developed an after-school program, so older children would have a place to go after school. Day-care centers are open long hours—from 6:30 A.M. to 6:00 P.M.—and parents are thus able to put in a full day's work without worrying about their children.

In rural areas, transportation becomes extremely difficult. Within the urban areas of the Roanoke Valley, it is a relatively simple matter to pick up preschoolers and bring them to the centers; when the distances involved become several miles, the complexities of transportation become overwhelming. For young children in the country who cannot take advantage of Head Start, TAP initiated a "Home Start" program.

In Home Start, a caseworker visits a rural family twice a week, explaining childhood development to the parents and helping the parents involve the child in educational activities and play. Home Start shows parents how to enrich the lives of their youngsters in order to prepare them for a more successful school career. When the time arrives for a Home Start child to enter school, he is already familiar with the alphabet, numbers, colors, and other basic elements of learning. Such preschool preparation is a novel idea for parents who did not experience it themselves; but it can do a lifetime of good for a young child and help break the pernicious cycle of rural poverty.

Since the Head Start program began, some of its functions have been taken over by public school kindergartens. However, TAP believes that the children of poverty need the individual attention that Head Start gives them. Children entering first grade from Head Start are more comfortable, more able to achieve, and more confident than non–Head Start children. Although studies of students in the early years of Head Start showed IQ gains in participating children, such gains seem to be temporary, and Head Start children eventually develop at a pace with their peers. The social gains, however, are long lasting, and Head Start before school begins can prevent a child from dropping out later.

Head Start works directly with potential welfare recipients and potential dropouts at the beginning of their lives. By changing the way children approach education, Head Start enables them to get more out of school and to stay there longer.

Youth Programs. The needs of poor children do not stop once they enter school. Head Start is a good beginning, but it is not enough. That is why TAP initiated several youth programs aimed at older children, intended to help them enter the mainstream of society. After-school care and summer day care, for example, are provided for grade-school children. The need for day care does not disappear when the child reaches school age, and many poor parents continue to use the TAP day-care facilities for their older children.

In 1966, TAP tried Operation Homework, a tutoring project to assist students after school. Another way TAP tried to further education was through a Dropout Mobile, a van that went around to poor neighborhoods, bringing staff members to talk dropouts into returning to school.

Beyond education, however, the primary needs of older children are for jobs and recreation, both of which structure the child's use of free time. Organized activities teach children to cooperate and to function as part of a larger entity.

A part-time job can keep a poor student from quitting school. If he can earn enough money to pay for books, supplies, and clothing, a poor student is much more likely to continue his education. In addition, exposure to a work environment brings home the real-life importance of an education; someone who is considering dropping out will tend to stay in school if he sees firsthand the benefits of a high-school diploma.

Over the years, there has been wide programming for youth from TAP. Three swimming pools were built in 1968 to provide extended recreational activities. A television program, *Operation Insight,* was broadcast on WBRA-TV in 1968 to help prepare the public for school desegregation; and student discussions and teacher training were conducted at William Fleming High School in 1971 to reduce racial tensions. A short-term jobs program to prepare young people for blue-collar work, Industry Bound, was started in 1971. In 1973, the Child Program Board was created to run group foster homes for adolescents.

It was not until 1975, though, that TAP established a Youth Services component under the direction of Jayne Thomas. Jayne, like many other TAP staffers, arrived in that position through an unconventional route. After several years of community action work in the area of training, Jayne quit her job in Indiana, took her 11-year-old son, and abruptly departed for Washington, D.C. It was 1972, and she needed to escape her husband, who was not taking her request for a divorce very amicably. Friends and associates in Washington tried to find her a job in community action, but none was found.

Finally, about to be evicted from her motel for lack of money, accompanied by the 11 year old who should have been in school, and near panicked after two unproductive weeks of job hunting, Jayne met with the director of the community action program in Alexandria, Virginia, a man rumored to have $12,000 for training programs. Although he had no job to offer her, he told her of a CAP in Roanoke, Virginia, that was heavily involved in training. Jayne had never heard of Roanoke, much less of TAP, but at her urging, the CAP director called Bristow while Jayne sat by, and she was interviewed over the telephone.

The training director, Ted Edlich, was out of the office,

and Bristow asked where they could reach her later in the day to discuss further the possibility of a job at TAP. She said that she would stay right there at the Alexandria CAP until Bristow called her back—her motel would not welcome her unless she had money in hand to pay her bill. Ted was far from enthusiastic about hiring an unknown, unseen quantity, but Bristow was, for some unexplained reason, determined to hire Jayne and pressured Ted into agreeing. The return phone call offered Jayne a two-month consulting job if she could be there in two days. Her only question was how to spell Roanoke. She was at TAP for the next 10 years.

In the spring of 1975, the Roanoke city manager asked Bristow, Charlene Chambers, and Wilma Warren to come to his office to discuss youth problems. His request carried more than the usual note of urgency: juvenile delinquency was an increasing problem in Roanoke, and the city manager had, that day, received an anonymous telephone call threatening a long, hot summer, a terrifying prospect for a community that had escaped the heavy street violence that had marred many city summers during the 1960s. Bristow asked Jayne, still in the training component, to come up with some background information on youth programs and policies in the Roanoke Valley. He then took her along to the meeting with the city manager, who asked TAP to come up with some demonstration youth programs for the summer. On their return to TAP, Bristow assigned this task— but no budget—to Jayne, who to this day does not know exactly where the money came from to pay for the program.

The most successful program of that summer, and possibly of all the TAP youth programs before or since, was Earn and Learn, which was geared to 11, 12, and 13 year olds who were not eligible for the normal Summer Youth Employment program. Earn and Learn participants were given special work permits by a sympathetic juvenile judge and spent the summer working half the day and playing the other half. Their jobs were community service types of activities; their play, enrichment activities, such as field trips, swimming, and baseball, which they would not otherwise have been able to pursue.

Each child was paid $15 per week, $10 of which they agreed to put in the bank. All the kids opened their own bank accounts and faithfully deposited their money each week. At the end of the summer, the best stores in Roanoke agreed to give the kids 20 to 25 percent discounts on merchandise if they produced cards showing they were returning to school in the fall. TAP organized shopping trips with children and parents. The children withdrew their money from the bank and personally selected their back-to-school merchandise. Comparative shopping had been the focus of one of the summer's play sessions, and the children learned their lesson well: never in the history of Roanoke had clothing fabrics been felt so thoroughly nor seams pulled so rigorously to ensure the quality of the goods being purchased. Not only did Earn and Learn keep these children off the streets (the long, hot summer never materialized), but it taught them valuable lessons about work, play, money management, and their ability to make wise decisions.

This and other TAP-sponsored youth programs were so successful that, at the end of the summer, Bristow created a Youth Services component. He put Jayne in charge and provided her the luxurious budget of $16,000 to cover her own salary and the youth programs. The $16,000 was accompanied by Bristow's comment that if Jayne thought the job was worth doing, she would develop alternative funding sources. In this he was right: in mid-1977, when Jayne moved on to another program, she had developed a component with a one-million-dollar annual budget collected from 22 different sources.

After 1975, when employment, education, and recreation programs were combined into the Youth Services component, TAP expanded its youth-oriented activities. Programs proliferated, spurred by delinquency prevention grants and staff made available through the Public Services Employment VISTA and CETA programs. In operation at the time were Latch-Key for children with working parents; youth activity centers; and movies, sports, and other recreational activities, including Wilderness Challenge, a wilderness survival skills program.

With budget problems and funding cuts, TAP has been forced to limit youth programming and concentrate primarily on employment and training needs of school-age youths. Over the years, however, TAP has given training and work experience to low-income youths, age 14 to 21, and provided an income that enabled participants to remain in school while enhancing the family income. And TAP has offered an introduction to the world of work, an introduction that often stimulated an interest in education, careers, and job skills.

TAP Youth Services adopted as its motto "Taking Youth Seriously," which reflects its commitment to meeting the real needs of underprivileged youths—education, recreation, and employment. Under the Alternative Education program, teachers provide individualized instruction and counseling for high-school students, helping them in a special, alternative atmosphere. The program has operated classrooms in each Roanoke city high school but focuses primarily on one special class in the Jefferson High School.

Project Recovery reaches dropouts and works to reenroll them in Roanoke schools. Participants also receive counseling at TAP. The educational setting provides individual attention that prepares students to reenter their home school or receive a G.E.D. certificate. The emphasis of the program is on academics, motivation, and coping with school. Although not all dropouts can be reached, some have been helped through this program.

Rent-A-Kid, an after-school and summer program, found odd jobs for youths between the ages of 15 and 18. The jobs, provided by community homeowners, included lawn mowing, window cleaning, house cleaning, and other house, yard, garden, and orchard work. The jobs, while not permanent or ongoing, gave young people a chance to earn extra money and accomplish useful tasks.

TAP's employment placement program attempts to match youths with available jobs in the community. The employment specialists seek information about job openings and develop slots within nonprofit agencies, local governments, and small neighborhood businesses.

A different sort of program was the shopping cart retrieval program, which organized youths into a business. They returned supermarket shopping carts abandoned in the community and offered to clean and repair damaged carts.

To help both young and old, TAP organized Aid to the Elderly, a program that put young people to work helping low-income senior citizens. During the summer, the students did yard work and other routine household maintenance tasks for older residents who were financially and physically unable to perform such work themselves.

In the education of low-income youth, TAP set up programs to help kids in school and give them organized activities after school.

The Latch-Key program provides children from 6 to 12 with a structured after-school program of creative arts, tutoring, field trips, recreation, and discussion groups. The children work closely with adult leaders and are able to influence the content of the activities. The program provides experience that helps poor children understand and participate in school activities, most of which are geared toward children with middle-class backgrounds.

TAP also organized art classes to enable low-income young people with talent to learn and practice the technical aspects of drawing. Students are referred by art teachers or other community leaders; the program gives individual attention and intensive instruction not otherwise available in art programs for the poor.

The Youth Volunteers program provides service for the

101

community and learning opportunities for young people by involving them in existing agencies as volunteers. In this way, they can become familiar with public agencies and their activities. The program also gives young people a chance to be helpers, rather than aid recipients.

The Gainsboro-Northwest Boys and Girls Club provides ongoing leadership for boys and girls between the ages of 8 and 15. Adult volunteers organize the children into activity groups; they take part in arts, crafts, field trips, community service work, personal hygiene classes, and tutorial activities. The leader is able to take a personal interest in each child and makes home and school visits to assess each child's progress and growth.

Reading skills are often a severe problem for poor children. Insufficient reading experience and poor educational achievement mean that poor children are not familiar with the idea of reading for pleasure. Reading is Fundamental encourages increased reading skills and provides books free of charge.

In recreational programs, TAP has set up, in response to community request, a weight-lifting program. TAP provides space, equipment, and instruction for impoverished youths who are interested in lifting weights.

During the summers, many children from middle-class homes go to camp. TAP operates a summer fresh-air camp to enable low-income youths to experience camping. An outdoor day camp, staffed mostly with volunteers, gives children a chance to participate in arts and crafts, hiking, basketball, baseball, horseshoes, and cookouts. The camp is located in a rural area, where children have a real outdoor experience, totally away from their inner-city homes.

In addition to other sports activities, TAP organized track, football, basketball, and baseball teams to compete across neighborhood lines, with meets held in various city parks. To provide weekly entertainment for neighborhood children, TAP organized a free summer movie program. Complete movie programs were shown each week at community centers and public housing projects.

Youth Services staff are interested in helping children grow through exposure to cultural experiences. In 1982, 200 children were taken to see *The Nutcracker Suite,* for many their first exposure to ballet. TAP has plans to make this event an annual affair.

The cycle of poverty can be broken at any point, but the group most vulnerable to change is the children. In order to reach the children, however, Youth Services has had to understand their special needs. TAP has long been a haven for young people, a place they can go whatever their problems, a place where they can receive caring and intelligent assistance. Hopelessness, loneliness, and fear affect children in poverty; TAP provides a refuge for poor youths who do not have any other resources.

TAP programs cover the time from preschool through high-school graduation. Underprivileged children need this comprehensive attention to encourage them to stay with a system that, to many of them, seems hostile and pointless.

Alienation is a common problem among young people. It is particularly damaging to a poor youth, who may feel (with some justification) that the school system and normal employment channels have nothing to offer him. TAP's youth programs help bring dropouts and impoverished young people back into the mainstream by providing jobs and recreational opportunities. Furthermore, the young people meet and work with successful adults who came from the same deprived backgrounds that they confront.

And that is one of the most influential aspects of the TAP youth programs: young people are able to see, in TAP staffers, people from poor backgrounds who are now working, earning money, and helping others.

5

GOING STRAIGHT

TAP gave me my space. That's what it's here for.
Lin Atkins, October 1979

AS THE FALL WINDS blew through Roanoke train yards in 1971, Lin Atkins huddled in a corner wondering whether she would live or die. She was not yet 21, a divorcee, and a drug addict. How bright the future seemed to her parents a few short years before, when she graduated from high school as valedictorian of her class, no doubt bound for college. What her parents did not know was that Lin hated her middle-class home and her middle-class school and her middle-class future. She followed a classic dropout pattern—the hasty marriage, the inevitable divorce, the lure of hard drugs, the mean streets, the ultimate choice. Lin Atkins decided to live.

It is again fall, eight years later. Lin sits in her office on Shenandoah Avenue and reads the riot act to a client over the phone, a crying alcoholic who sobs that the world is crashing in and that booze is the only thing that can help him. "Don't give me that shit, you son of a bitch. You get your ass over there and get dried out." She knows all the excuses only too well.

Her office walls, like many at TAP, are plastered with mementos and statements. A horoscope plaque certifies that Lin is a Leo; a poster urges "Jobs, not Jails"; there are numerous certificates and awards from workshops; and there are pictures of Lin with prison inmates. For Lin Atkins is now the director of TAP's ex-offender programs.

The road back was not easy. There was detoxification at Southwestern State; the Rubicon drug program in Richmond; a job at Hegira House in Roanoke, a halfway house for addicts trying to go straight. Finally, in 1974, she went to work in TAP's training division and was drawn inevitably into ex-offender work. Now she says, "TAP gave me my space. That's what it's here for."

Poverty and the Ex-offender

America incarcerates a higher percentage of its citizens than any other Western democracy, and the number of persons in jail is constantly increasing. Each year, state and local governments allot more and more money to the building and maintenance of prisons. Millions of dollars are pumped into the criminal justice system, yet the crime rate does not decrease.

One reason for this failure is that so-called correctional institutions do not, in fact, correct anything. They are purely punitive, requiring an offender to "do time" in proportion to the purported severity of his offense, while offering no assistance in overcoming the problems that led to crime in the first place. Prisons are merely holding facilities, keeping the prisoners for a period and then releasing them, either unchanged or actively damaged, back into the community. Ninety-five percent of those in prison are eventually returned to their communities. Of those, between one-third and one-half will commit another crime and return to prison. One estimate holds that 80 percent of all crime is committed by recidivist prisoners.

Prisons do not prepare an offender for life on the outside. Prisoners live in a tightly controlled, tightly confined, rigidly structured environment, one in which any form of self-reliance, independence, or initiative is punished rather than rewarded. An offender who is sent to prison adapts to a situation that is totally unlike his former life and, importantly, also unlike his life after release. Prisoners who

105

have served sentences of several years become adjusted to life behind bars and unable to cope with the rigors of independent living. Some cases of recidivism are directly and obviously motivated by a desire to return to prison.

Studies of "transition shock" show that it can take from 6 to 18 months to bottom out and begin a real adjustment to life on the outside. Normal parole supervision decreases after several months, just when a released prisoner may be suffering the worst crisis of returning to life on the outside. The adjustment from prison to the outside may be so stressful that a prisoner returns to crime from anxiety or because it is the only way he knows to exist. Here is Cabell Brand on the subject:

> In Virginia, a prisoner returns to the community with no more than $25 in his pocket. If his home is out of state, he is given a ticket to the state line. A small percentage of prisoners have families to provide shelter, some income, and emotional support until they get on their feet. Most are unwelcome and unwanted by family, former employers, and the community at large. Housing, clothing, transportation, food, and emergency funds are real and immediate needs. No longer are prisoners required to have a job before release, and with unemployment over 8.4 percent, jobs take awhile to land, even for the most conscientious. For those who do not have families, churches, or employers ready to give them a hand, there is a ready-made, 24-hour-a-day support system available: the street. The corner hangouts of those who are engaged in criminal activity, who can supply immediate cash, a pad, a gig, drugs, companionship, a good time, and a road back to prison. The major causes of recidivism are financial need, low self-esteem, and peer support. The street supplies all three.

But the ex-offender is not the only one who suffers; families of prisoners suffer in equal measure. The families of incarcerated criminals are frequently poor, and the link between crime and poverty is well-established. When one member of a family, particularly the breadwinner, is put into prison, the family is severely disrupted. They may have to go on welfare or find other, supplementary income to keep going. In addition, there is the humiliation and debasement of dealing with an impersonal and uncaring criminal justice system. Families of prisoners need help in adjusting to life during and after incarceration; divorce is common when a spouse is imprisoned. Yet the family is particularly important for the adjustment of prisoners after release. The recidivism rate for married ex-offenders is considerably lower than that for those who are single and therefore likely to feel isolated.

In 1975, a group of concerned criminal justice and social service professionals approached TAP about the need for a reentry program aimed at released prisoners. The caseloads of parole officers and probation officials were too large to allow for adequate assistance to prisoners looking for work, housing, or transportation. There was no allowance for provision of social services to families of prisoners, and recidivism was a major problem.

Early Ex-offender Program

In the past, the TAP staff had been involved with drug therapy groups conducted at Botetourt Correctional Center #25 in Troutville, Virginia. Because of their interaction with these programs, and with the participants, the TAP staff became aware that prisoners had virtually no programs or assistance being offered to them upon their release. Ex-offender programs were structured to offset this lack of resources.

A proposal submitted to the Comprehensive Employment and Training Agency (CETA) resulted in funding for the Stop-Gap jobs program. Stop-Gap provided interim employment for newly released inmates. Since that time, TAP has also initiated Virginia CARES, a pre- and post-release counseling and employment training program; Prison Families, designed to help families cope with the strains of having an incarcerated relative; Friends to Victims of Crime, a service for low-income crime victims; and WINGS, a theater program designed to enrich the lives of inmates.

These programs continued TAP's policy of investigating nontraditional means of dealing with complex social problems. The offender programs exemplify TAP's unusual approach to poverty assistance. Prisoners, who are often poor, are not normally included in poverty action programs: they do not fit the traditional "deserving poor" model. The criminal system is merely punitive, and ex-offenders are ignored by many social assistance programs.

TAP recognized the depressing and repetitive pattern of many convicts' lives. An individual will commit a crime, go to jail, and, possibly, leave a family unsupported. The family, in addition to being deprived of income from the incarcerated member, may be overwhelmed with legal bills. For periods of up to several years, the family must cope with multiple stresses: shame, debt, and social stigma. When the ex-offender is released, if he does not rejoin his family, he has nowhere to go. Finding a job is difficult, not only because of a criminal record, but because the average prisoner has no high-school diploma and reads at the fifth-grade level. The exconvict is likely to commit another crime, and the cycle begins again.

TAP believes it is possible to break the cycle and to help an ex-offender stay out of jail and lead a productive life. TAP's ex-offender programs give people counseling in dealing with job and family problems and a caring, supportive atmosphere to ease the transition from life in prison to life in the world.

Stop-Gap. The CETA-funded Stop-Gap jobs program began in 1976 and worked at providing a controlled transitional period between jail and a full return to society. This "stop-gap" period lasted only three months, but it provided a unique temporary employment period for 10 to 12 enrollees in each cycle. The program also provided supportive services and life-coping skills. It began with an intense 2-week orientation period followed by 10 weeks of on-the-job experience. After three months, participants were placed in permanent jobs, training programs, or school.

The main function of the Stop-Gap program is providing an employment-like situation for the released convict. Participants learn to adjust to a regular schedule, keeping specified hours and regulating their own activities. In addition, work in the Stop-Gap program brings ex-offenders into contact with employers, educates them on how to prepare a job resume, how to fill out job applications, and how to conduct themselves appropriately during an interview. Matters of money management and personal problems are also covered in counseling, and the ex-convict is given a framework on which to build a productive existence. Stop-Gap participants work in one of three main job programs: Storefront, Job Research, and Community Education.

Storefront workers deal with other ex-offenders within the CETA system, as well as talking to clients on a walk-in basis. They provide peer counseling, job counseling, help in developing job readiness skills, and assistance in compiling resumes. In addition, they perform outreach and follow-up for all offender programs administered by TAP.

Participants in Job Research make initial contacts with prospective employers and determine each employer's attitude toward hiring ex-offenders. Job Research has educated employers and dispelled many of the myths that frequently hinder opportunities for ex-offenders. The Job Research Bank lists about 350 local companies, all of whom are contacted regularly about possible openings.

Community Education participants contact civic organizations, social clubs, businessmen, and churches in order to set up speaking engagements. In this way, the community is kept informed about the life styles, personalities, needs, and attitudes of ex-offenders.

The flexibility and creativity of the program allowed staff to create other employment opportunities if the client so desired. Some ex-offenders worked in the weatherization, maintenance, Head Start, and Youth programs.

In the years between 1976 and 1981, Stop-Gap enrolled 267 participants. Of these, 155 were placed in gainful employment; an additional 55 returned to school or were placed in training programs. Stop-Gap's recidivism rate is around 8 percent, and graduates have shown a 56 percent retention rate in keeping their jobs. When many graduates do leave their positions, it is to move on to a better job with higher pay.

Stop-Gap served as a model for other programs, including Project Breakthrough in Lynchburg. It was also instrumental in the early development of Virginia CARES, discussed later.

Today, after an inmate is released, there are post-release programs throughout Virginia that assist ex-offenders in obtaining housing, jobs, transportation, family and individual counseling, and emergency funds. Virginia CARES has been responsible for the development of three temporary employment programs in Roanoke, Lynchburg, and Alexandria. These programs have provided three months of employment, like the Stop-Gap program, for those who have the most difficulty in making the transition.

Inmates Program. With the support of the Virginia Department of Corrections, TAP has run three volunteer programs at Botetourt Correctional Unit #25, a road camp. A self-awareness group, run for 8 to 10 inmates by two TAP staff leaders, focuses on behavior theories, experimental training, and interaction. TAP does not expect inmates to benefit from forced change; these groups suggest to inmates that experience has provided limited life choices, but that there are alternatives available. In addition, a G.E.D. program uses volunteers and hired staff to prepare inmates for the high-school-equivalency exam. A self-supporting arts and crafts program produced articles for sale at area craft fairs; part of the money is turned back for new materials, and the rest goes into accounts for the inmates involved.

The Prison Families program was set up to help the families of prisoners. In many cases, a convict is sent to a prison far from his home, and it is difficult for family members and friends to visit. In the Prison Families program, families are brought together to give each other support. They are counseled to help them to live as normally as possible during the family member's incarceration. Transportation is provided to spouses and friends for prison visits. For some, this means traveling several hours over distances they could not afford to travel independently. Families in need of other family-related social services are referred to agencies that provide the necessary help.

TAP also runs a self-awareness counseling program for the inmates of the Roanoke City and Roanoke County jails. Sessions are held twice a week with the objective of breaking down barriers between inmates, building a support system while they are incarcerated, and referring them to transition-assistance programs once they are released.

TAP's Inmate Legal Assistance program offers a liaison between prisoners and volunteer attorneys. No criminal cases are handled by this program, which treats only civil problems. The program is cosponsored with the Young Lawyers Conference of the State Bar, which initiated it in 1977.

The Inmate Job Readiness, Development, and Placement project provides prerelease job motivation training, job development and placement, and related services to inmates. The grantees, along with TAP, are the Richmond Community Action Program, the Southeastern Tidewater Opportunity Project, and the Virginia Employment Commission. Programs are operated within 12 state correctional institutions.

WINGS. Possibly the most creative and innovative program for inmate rehabilitation was WINGS, a theater/drama/improvisation workshop for prisoners in different Virginia state correctional facilities.

The project began with an idea by Jere Lee Hodgins and Jim Ayers of the Mill Mountain Playhouse in Roanoke. They conceived a plan to bring theater to prison inmates and approached Ted Edlich of TAP. Edlich, in turn, consulted Lin Atkins, the head of TAP's offender programs, who also became enthusiastic over the project. WINGS was eventually funded by a grant from the culture section of the American Correctional Association.

In September 1977, four professional performers were hired and began rehearsals and human relations training. On October 24 of that year, WINGS presented its first show, "Gimmeabreak," for inmates of the Staunton, Virginia, prison. The original improvisational play was performed twice, once in the afternoon and again in the evening. After each performance, the company stayed around to answer questions and to describe the workshops that were being offered. Twenty men signed up, and workshops began the following day.

Acting workshops were held every Wednesday and Thursday from nine to four over a two-month period. At first, inmates worked with the professional actors in theater games and exercises designed to teach them techniques of improvisation and acting. Gradually, the inmates worked more and more on their own, with the addition of constructive criticism and encouragement from the WINGS company.

On December 15, the group put on a performance for their fellow inmates and the prison staff. As a result of the WINGS program, inmates decided to continue work on their own, and formed their own performance group, Feathers.

E. W. Murray, superintendent of the Staunton Correctional Center, said about the program: "Because the Staunton Correctional Center is treatment-oriented, I feel the proj-

112

ect has given another dimension to our endeavors to provide the residents with means of self-expression. The value of knowing oneself is too often pushed into the background for incarcerated individuals. Participation in the theatrical field tends to act as a vehicle for expression, a socially acceptable outlet, which is very therapeutic....I would like to see your project continued at Staunton."

WINGS moved next to the Virginia Correctional Center for Women in Goochland, Virginia. The overall objectives for the program remained the same as for the Staunton workshops, but the design of the individual sessions and some of the material chosen for performance were changed to reflect the difference in this participating group. Women who performed in the program also eventually formed an independent group, called Tips, and set up a touring exchange program with the Staunton group. One of the women inmates who participated described the program by saying, "There is one thing of joy which I look forward to each week. It breaks the boredom, relieves tensions, is a lot of fun, plus is something very positive. What I'm talking about is our theater group every Tuesday evening."

The theater workshops at Bland Correctional Center, in Bland, Virginia, were structured like those at Staunton and Goochland. Again, new plays were added to the WINGS repertoire. The Bland facility already had a drama club in existence, so no additional WINGS-related group formed. However, several WINGS participants were drama club members, so the techniques learned through the WINGS workshops were carried over into club productions.

Prison theater workshops go beyond simple cultural enrichment. They show the value of time and encourage internal discipline in learning lines, exercising, singing, and practicing. Prisoners learn to examine themselves in new ways and find resources within themselves of which they had been unaware. Not only do the plays entertain, they promote growth, change, and awareness. And workshop

113

participants tend to cooperate better with their fellow prisoners. The number of "incidents" involving WINGS participants was considerably lower than before the workshops.

Virginia CARES

The average released prisoner walks out of jail with no place to go. He typically is black, young, male, poor, and uneducated. His family relationships are weak; he has never held a steady job and lacks the skills to do so. He has not completed high school and reads at the fifth- to eighth-grade level. This "average" prisoner is likely to return to the environment he knew before his incarceration, the same environment that led him to crime in the first place. When he faces the multiple problems that adjustment to life outside prison entails, he is likely to commit another crime and be returned to jail.

Virginia CARES (Community Action Re-Entry System) works before and after release to give the prisoner skills necessary to return to the community. In a very real sense, the program is in competition with life on the street. It must divert the prisoner away from returning to his criminal life style. Its essence is retraining: retraining a person who knows only one side of society to live on the other side.

Virginia CARES is probably the most ambitious of TAP's ex-offender programs. The concept developed from TAP's ex-offender work, and Virginia CARES now serves as the statewide ex-offender reorientation program. It operates through a network of 21 community action agencies working with the prisoner population of Virginia.

Virginia ranks 13th among states in the nation in total prison population. The per-capita rate, however, is much higher. At any one time, approximately 9,000 adult prisoners are behind bars. Prison construction and maintenance alone cost the commonwealth $250 million every year. The system of criminal incarceration tends to be self-perpetuating: approximately 34 percent of those released are returned to prison within three years. At least 9 percent will be returned to prison within a year.

In 1978, the executive directors and staff from 15 community action agencies in Virginia met to plan an offender assistance program. A proposal to the Governor's Employment and Training Council led to a prerelease program in 5 institutions. During the next two years, it expanded to 20. The program has staff teams from 4 community action agencies enter each institution and provide 30-hour workshops on self-awareness, decision-making skills, job motivation skills, and making the transition into society.

The "inside" part of the program involves prisoners who are 6 to 12 months away from their release date. A combination of group workshops and individual counseling sessions focuses on what the prisoner can expect once he is released. Topics stressed include normal skills for coping with life, such as acquiring a driver's license, opening a bank account, shopping sensibly, and managing one's personal finances. In addition, there is intense preparation for a job search. Volunteers and prerelease staff work with prisoners in filling out sample job applications, preparing resumes, participating in simulated employment interviews, and other job-related tasks. The prisoners work together in group workshops and private sessions. They are given evaluations of their performance in the areas of instruction and guidance in how to improve their skills.

The prerelease program helps a prisoner foresee what problems he is likely to face once released and, with this knowledge, plan ahead to solve them.

When a prisoner is released, a Virginia CARES staff member from one of the participating community action agencies greets him. The staff worker will help him find lodging, food, and suitable clothing. In prison, all the basics

115

are provided at no cost, of time or energy, to the inmate. Virginia CARES takes the first step with the ex-offender, helping him discover how to take care of himself.

If the exconvict has a family, the Virginia CARES worker will get together with social workers to help deal with family problems. If necessary, they will arrange for counseling to help the family make it through the initial, difficult adjustments. Statistics show that an exprisoner who stays with his family is much less likely to return to prison.

Once the immediate needs of the prisoner are met, the focus shifts to finding employment. This step is one of the most important in the postrelease program. There is widespread prejudice in the job market against exconvicts, and when unemployment is high, there is little chance that someone whose main work experience has been in a prison laundry will be able to find a job.

Virginia CARES counsels the exprisoner in job-finding techniques and provides moral support. Workers track down job leads and create jobs by approaching sympathetic local businesses. The Virginia CARES staff members approach potential employers, offering an evaluation of the ex-offender's skills, abilities, and personality. After an ex-offender has been placed, follow-up visits let him know that he is not forgotten and that the system has not abandoned him.

Virginia CARES has been responsible for the development of three temporary employment programs in Roanoke, Lynchburg, and Alexandria. These programs provide three months of temporary employment, specifically for those ex-offenders who have had greater difficulty than usual in making the transition from prison to freedom. The program, based on the Stop-Gap jobs program started by TAP, provides controlled work experience in an understanding environment.

Virginia CARES currently has only 20 postrelease staff members working in 33 counties and 19 cities. Considering the overall size of the prison population, this is obviously insufficient. Volunteers, an essential part of the program, help pick up the slack. These volunteers teach prisoners job application skills, consumer education, and how to fill out some of the forms they are likely to need on the outside.

Virginia CARES is an important answer to the crime problem. Studies indicate that as much as 80 percent of all crime is committed by repeat offenders. If a program such as Virginia CARES can reduce the recidivism rate by even a few percentage points, it would, not only reduce the amount of crime committed, but also reduce the number of prisoners. Confining criminals in prisons is an expensive, ineffective approach to many aspects of the crime problem. The incarceration of larger and larger segments of the population merely keeps them out of the criminal pool for the duration of their sentence; it does nothing to reduce the likelihood of their committing another crime. The Virginia CARES program retrains prisoners so that they need not return to the lives that led them to prison.

In spite of the potential financial savings to the state of a reduced prison population, Virginia CARES suffers from chronic underfunding. (In 1982, the budget was augmented by a grant from the Ford Foundation to keep the Virginia CARES services in operation until the state budget was released in July.) However, the potential financial benefits of prisoner rehabilitation programs are enormous. Every prisoner costs the state between $11,000 and $15,000 a year. If the prison population were reduced by only a few thousand, the reduction in state expenses would be enormous.

TAP believes that a program such as Virginia CARES, if applied statewide, could significantly reduce crime. The interrelated problems of recidivism and poverty, which make one-time prisoners into multiple offenders, must be attacked. Virginia CARES goes after these problems.

Part of the reason for the success of TAP programs is that they are voluntary. The amount of assistance a person gets depends on his willingness to accept it; the amount of progress he makes depends on his willingness to work at moving forward. There are endless opportunities for a newly released ex-offender to slide back into his old patterns, and it is impossible to force someone to change his life. The desire must come from within.

One way TAP encourages prisoners to make the effort is by making the options attractive, by demonstrating that other ways of life are not only possible but preferable. One of TAP's best advertisements for life reform is in the person of Lin Atkins. An ex-offender herself, she began at TAP as a Stop-Gap worker and eventually worked her way up to program director on the permanent staff. By using people like Lin as outreach workers and counselors, TAP's programs display a better understanding of the problems of prisoners. It is impossible for someone who has not been in prison to understand what it is like, and TAP's workers are able to approach rehabilitation from the standpoint of a person who has been through the system. TAP's workers can detect the manipulation and evasion that characterize relationships in prison. Someone with less direct experience might be taken advantage of, but an exconvict knows how the scams work.

Another advantage of the TAP programs, and similar independent community action agency programs, is that they are not part of the prison system. Prisoners tend to see their probation officer as an adversary and a threat, a person to be hoodwinked, lied to, and manipulated in any way possible. To a released prisoner, the parole officer is merely one more variation of the prison guard, a person placed in authority over the offender to curtail his liberty. Parole interviews become a game: What can the parolee get away with? What can be hidden from the guard?

For this reason, programs of prisoner rehabilitation set up within the correctional system are less likely to work. Prisoners who come to TAP for help trust TAP precisely because it is outside the system. TAP's workers are obviously not ordinary correctional system employees, are not guards or police or officials, but instead may be exconvicts themselves, working to help their peers. Although the government funds the program, it is because the government does not run it that the program is effective.

In the end, one of the most persuasive arguments in favor of prisoner rehabilitation is cost. Reducing recidivism, even by a small percentage, is amazingly cost-effective, since it costs upwards of $12,000 a year to keep a prisoner in jail. And as the prison population grows, so grows the need for new prisons and more personnel.

Building, maintaining, and running a large prison system is expensive. If the number of ex-offenders returning to prison could be reduced, the need for more prison space would be reduced. The long-term saving realized by funding a comprehensive prisoner reeducation and training program would more than offset the cost of such a program; reducing recidivism by even a small percentage would eventually cut the prison population by many thousands.

The fact remains that, as it stands, the current correctional system does not correct, nor does it rehabilitate. Prisons are simply a way of keeping antisocial elements away from society; they do nothing toward solving the real cause of criminal behavior.

By reducing crime, TAP's Virginia CARES and Stop-Gap jobs programs benefit, not only the individuals who participate, but the community. A major concern of city residents is street crime; if TAP programs put a dent in the constantly growing crime rate, they serve the entire city. A former prisoner who has been enabled to find and keep a job is one side of the success story of TAP's prisoner programs. The other side is the street that is just a little safer, the family that did not suffer at the hands of a criminal, and the prison system that is just a little less crowded than it would have been without TAP.

119

6

TAP WATER

The number of water taps per 1,000 population will be an infinitely more meaningful health indicator than the number of hospital beds.

Halfdan Mahler, Director-General, World Health Organization

FOR MOST AMERICANS, drinking water, and water for other personal uses, such as bathing and cleaning, is not a problem. They turn the tap and there it is, not particularly tasty and probably smelling slightly of chlorine, but free of bacteria and in plentiful supply. The average American uses 75 gallons of water per day. The greatest water problems for most people are likely to be bans on car washing and lawn watering in periods of extreme drought.

The disposal of wastewater is also likely to be a routine matter of life in these United States. The flush toilet, the kitchen sink, and the bathroom drain carry household wastes (99 percent of which is water) to city sewers and suburban septic tanks (over which the grass always grows greener). All this water and wastewater is routed through a system of pipes called indoor plumbing, a housing feature that has become a kind of symbol of modern industrial sociey. The decennial U.S. census, however, still collects information on households that do not have plumbing. There were nearly 1.8 million such households in 1980.

This figure identifies only the hard core of deprived users, the people who use the gas station across the road or "walk to privies in the rain," the people who haul water in five-gallon cans from distant places or buy water sold in Coke bottles. It does not identify the people who do the wash at

120

four in the morning because there is not enough water pressure at peak hours in the evening, the people whose back yards are filled with raw wastewater because their septic tanks do not function properly. When all these things are added in, it can easily be argued that 20 million Americans have an inadequate water supply and wastewater disposal system.

And who are these people? First of all, they are found mostly in rural areas and the forgotten fringes of small cities. Urban water may taste funny, but it is usually adequate in quality and quantity; the flush toilets may play havoc with the environment, but at least they work. Secondly, the people are mostly poor. Technology is not, per se, a problem. The engineers know how to find a water source, how to deliver water to households, how to treat water to make it safe for consumption and wastewater to make it safe for disposal. The trick is to do all these things at a price people can afford. Wealthy people in rural areas have no water problems they cannot solve; they simply pay whatever it costs to install the necessary facilities.

Thus, it is poor people, by and large, who bear the burden of poor water and sanitation. Their children suffer from diarrhea, dysentery, impetigo, and a host of other water-related diseases, including occasional bouts with typhoid fever. It is their children who regularly must be wormed, much as dogs are wormed. Of course, adults suffer from water-related diseases too, but their systems adjust to most bad water conditions short of epidemics. Rural people often do not know that they have poor water. "The water's OK, just as long as you let it settle" is a statement frequently heard.

Although water and sanitation are poverty problems, they were not commonly addressed by community action agencies. One reason is the lack of public awareness of the problem. Another is the nature of the problem. Improving water and wastewater service usually involves the installation of facilities. Thus, in the early years, water projects were seen as "hardware" projects, more appropriate for engineers than poverty warriors.

Finally, the typical poverty program was "client-centered," that is, geared to help only needy individuals or families. Many water projects, of necessity, involve community facilities that provide service to all residents regardless of income. The funding agencies for water and sewer systems were not hard-hitting "poor people" agencies like OEO but traditional bureaucracies with banker mentalities. The Farmers Home Administration (FmHA) in the U.S. Department of Agriculture was the chief such agency.

For all these reasons, community action agencies (CAAs) tended to overlook water and sanitation as areas for the application of service, advocacy, and reform techniques. One CAA that did not was TAP.

Demonstration Water Project

In 1968, residents of five counties surrounding Roanoke met under TAP auspices to discuss their water problems. They decided to establish a separate organization and seek OEO funding to improve water service for low-income people in the five-county area. The new corporation was christened Demonstration Water Project (DWP). All five counties had representatives on the board of directors.

DWP received a demonstration grant from OEO and began operation in 1969. The board chose an outsider, Joe Van Deventer, as executive director, but former TAP staffers played a key role in the new organization. Ed Weingard was responsible for field work; J. C. Reynolds handled training; Elaine Stinson dealt with finance and administration; Wally Johnston was construction supervisor.

In the TAP service area as elsewhere, the problem was mainly one of delivery. There was plentiful water in subterranean aquifers waiting to be tapped. The technology for reaching the water and bringing it out in usable quantities was well known and easily available. But thousands of families did not have the organization, the knowledge, or, most importantly, the money to enable wells to be drilled and water to be pumped into their homes.

The basic methodology of Demonstration Water Project was simple. DWP would identify rural communities with severe water problems, organize groups to deal with these problems, and help the communities develop water projects by securing loans, obtaining official approval, and contributing engineering services. DWP helped with all the skills needed to complete a complex system of water treatment. The water systems themselves, when complete, were intended to be run by volunteers from the community. This would keep the rates for service low and within the reach of the poor families the system was intended to serve. Volunteers from the service area would be trained in management, operation, and maintenance of their own water system.

Thus, a major part of the Demonstration Water Project's purpose was to foster community organization and development, as well as to provide drinkable water and effective waste disposal. DWP therefore required a broad degree of citizen participation in all aspects of planning, construction, and organization. FmHA also played a key role. The standard financial "package" in DWP-developed projects was mostly FmHA money—50 percent loan, 30 percent grant—with DWP/OEO funds making up the balance.

DWP's work became something of a model in the water and sewer development process because a logical sequence of steps was always followed. First, the target community—say, Delaney Court or Southern Hills—was identified through a "needs assessment process."

Requests for assistance originated from communities themselves or were referred by state, federal, or other agencies. The income levels of the residents, the number of people affected, the history of efforts to solve the problem, and the type of assistance required all were taken into account to identify specific needs and eligibility for assistance. In addition, training sessions were held for community leaders, and processes were discussed by which the community could solve the problem. Various plans and means of construction and ownership were proposed and considered, with input from the community a vital part of this step.

Next, preliminary plans were made. These could include establishing a community association, holding public hearings, selecting an engineer to investigate the problem, and preparing funding and project applications. The activities at this stage included forming an operating entity, which could take the form of a nonprofit association, water district, public service district, or some other public service administrative organization incorporated in some way. An engineer was selected at this stage, and preliminary engineering plans were drawn up. The problems were brought to the attention of appropriate officials, and the preliminary engineering study was reviewed.

With the preliminary work in hand, the community sought financing commitments. In this step, training assistance from the local community action agency was required, since many communities were inexperienced in funding and development grantsmanship. The economic feasibility of the project and the ability of the target community to repay its loans were tested at this stage.

The community organization received training in submission of financing documentation, approaches to organizing users of the system, and record keeping and funds accountability. Obviously, this milestone was an important one; at this point, a major commitment was made to complete the project. When documentation confirming commitment of at least 50 percent of the funds required for total project financing was received, the project could proceed.

This required drawing up the final plans and specifications. Community action participation included assistance with strategies for obtaining easements and rights-of-way and for complying with federal and state regulations. Engineering drawings were completed at this stage, as were bid specifications, security requirements, insurance, and bonding.

At this stage, contract negotiations for a bid award were undertaken. All phases of construction, from preconstruction conferences to final inspection of the project, were finished at this stage. Community action participation here included liaison between community leaders and construction personnel and assistance to low-income residents in obtaining linkage to the water system.

After initial advertising for bids, which was required to comply with government regulations, the bids were tabulated and one was accepted by the community and funding source. The construction contracts were then awarded, and conferences were held with the funding agencies, engineer, contractors, and attorneys. Now the system could be constructed, inspected, completed, and accepted by the community, lenders, and owners.

Finally, an operation and maintenance plan was developed, and the system was put into operation, usually after a ribbon-cutting ceremony.

Using this methodology, Demonstration Water Project developed water systems in 10 different communities. DWP also brought water facilities to individual families in isolated rural locations, such as Franklin County. These homes were too isolated for an effective community system and needed private wells. A combination of DWP grants, loans, and FmHA assistance enabled many low-income rural houses to have decent, safe water.

The Demonstration Water Project was an autonomous corporation, set up by TAP, staffed with many people who came from TAP, but having its own board of directors and its own corporate structure. It was, like most TAP programs, self-help oriented. The goal was to train and organize communities to own, run, and maintain their water systems independently. This training included administrative instruction for board members from the community, technical training for staff, and financial instruction for officers.

The end result of a Demonstration Water Project program was, ideally, a self-sustaining corporation. The corporation would set rates, collect the money, and run the system on its own. Again, this follows in the TAP tradition of establishing a program that later would run on its own.

The water project showed the potential for being adopted on a wider basis, and DWP approached OEO in 1971 with suggestions for broadening its base of operations. Early in 1972, DWP received a $6 million, three-year grant to conduct a national program that would replicate the Roanoke area experience.

The national project, called (eventually) National Demonstration Water Project, would find community action and other social program agencies in other areas of the country and let these organizations play the same role in water project development as played by TAP and its Demonstration Water Project. National Demonstration Water Project (NDWP) became incorporated in 1973, with headquarters in Washington, D.C. The organization quickly set out to look for other projects in other states to participate in this national program. NDWP took steps toward setting up a national network of low-income agencies to participate in water development programs.

Meanwhile, the Demonstration Water Project in Roanoke was changing. Some of the theories that had been formulated for use in rural areas did not work out. For example, the passage of the Safe Drinking Water Act in 1974 brought stricter drinking water standards and made some features of the DWP programs obsolete. Volunteer operators were no longer adequate for most systems, and DWP realized that there was an increased need for trained, professional system operators.

In 1975, TAP essentially "reclaimed" DWP, reorganized it, and reincorporated it as Virginia Water Project. Virginia Water Project remains a separate organization from TAP and remains an affiliate of National Demonstration Water Project, working in cooperation with other NDWP affiliates nationwide.

Virginia Water Project

Since 1975, VWP has worked throughout the state as the driving force in a network of community action agencies, other community-based organizations, and local government officials. The network approach makes it easier for local organizations to identify water and wastewater-related problems and to implement solutions. Since 1969, over 20,000 low-income rural Virginians have received, for the first time, safe drinking water or sanitary facilities or both. The network approach has created 140 projects in 112 communities.

Other agency projects, funded through special grants, have enabled VWP to broaden its ability to handle rural development and water needs. For example, the Small Town Emphasis Project (STEP) focused on rural housing, transportation, energy, health care, and economic development, as well as on water and wastewater facility development.

In its work with 11 rural Virginia communities, STEP helped identify local problems, generate low-cost innovative solutions, and improve local abilities to deal effectively with problems. Among the results of Virginia STEP activities have been a nonprofit fuel alcohol plant in Floyd County, a prenatal clinic for low-income women in Washington County, and a test of solar greenhouses and commercial composting toilets in the Nelson County community of Piney River.

127

Because of VWP's experience in rural resident participation, the U.S. Environmental Protection Agency (EPA) funded VWP to work in five rural Virginia communities that were then planning for wastewater treatment facilities. Staff services included training, technical assistance, education, and community organizing skills, which helped rural officials obtain more diverse citizen representation and greater citizen input into the facility planning process.

Another VWP project, Water Supply Contamination Notification, was funded by the Virginia Environmental Endowment and produced a handbook for use by local officials during drinking water contamination emergencies, such as spills of toxic chemicals or fuel oil. The handbook teaches local governments how to quickly and effectively notify the public during these crises. It has been distributed to every publicly owned water system in the state.

In 1980, the United Nations tagged the eighties as the International Drinking Water Supply and Sanitation Decade, with the goal of "safe drinking water and adequate sanitation for all by 1990." VWP was active in the establishment in 1981 of Global Water, a private, voluntary organization dedicated to implementing this goal in the United States and to improving and conserving water supplies worldwide.

VWP also administers the Southeast Rural Community Assistance Project (SE/R-CAP), which provides services to promote rural water and wastewater facility development in the states of Maryland, Delaware, North Carolina, South Carolina, Georgia, and Florida. SE/R-CAP is one of six regional technical resource centers nationwide that addresses rural water and wastewater problems. The centers were funded originally by the Community Services Administration (CSA) but, since 1981, are handled by the U.S. Department of Health and Human Services. Although each has its own structure and methods for achieving its particular objective, the goal of the regional centers is the same—to improve the water and wastewater service delivered to rural communities.

Since 1979, SE/R-CAP has developed a network of community-based organizations, local government bodies, and community action agencies in SE/R-CAP's seven-state region. As a result, 35 communities have initiated development activities. These activities will ultimately provide 12,000 new connections, benefiting 27,000 rural residents, of whom 34 percent will be low income. To date, these projects have leveraged $9,464,441 from public and private sources.

The SE/R-CAP central office staff is complemented by the staffs of over 175 community organizations throughout the Southeast. They provide a variety of services at no cost to the community, including on-site technical assistance, training, financing assistance, information, and engineering review services.

The moving force behind VWP is unquestionably Wilma Warren. Veteran observers predict that if there is ever a water project on the moon, it will be developed by Wilma. Her background does not fit the I've-been-there pattern at all, demonstrating again that the "TAP style" accommodates many individual styles. She was raised in Bridgewater, Virginia, in a warm and loving family, attended Bridgewater College, married, and had four children. When she and her family came to Roanoke in 1955, it appeared that her life style would follow a traditional pattern.

But Wilma became involved in civil rights issues in the late fifties and acquired a taste for social battles. When, in 1961, personal circumstances forced her to look for a job, it was Bristow Hardin, principal of West End Elementary School, who hired her as a secretary. When Bristow moved to TAP, he prevailed upon Wilma (she was hesitant) to come also as the first of his hires.

Beginning as a secretary-bookkeeper, Wilma eventually became Bristow's eyes and ears, a weather vane of needs and programs, a trouble-shooting member of the "inner sanctum." Although she applied for the executive director post when Bristow died, she actually supported Ted for the job, and she continued to work with him as she had with Bristow.

Although Wilma was never involved with DWP, Ted tapped her to head VWP soon after the new corporation was established. The rest, as they say, is history; the organization has been a major social program force in the state, in the southeastern region, and even nationally. The universe of development, however, may not be exhausted, as VWP's international interests indicate. Perhaps the moon is not as far-fetched as it sounds.

The local to state to regional to national progress of the water project is an outstanding example of the breadth of TAP's involvement in community action. The water project has accomplished, over the years of its operation and under its various names and affiliations, two separate goals.

In the first place, Demonstration Water Project and Virginia Water Project have assisted communities directly with water and wastewater system improvements. Money and technical assistance provided by these programs have enabled small, low-income, rural communities to improve the quality of life for their residents. Seed money for development and grants for hardware system construction have started the projects. And in the typical TAP manner, no program was completely controlled from the outside. In every case, community participation was an essential part of the development and construction process.

In the second place, the water project has caused political reform by making legislatures aware of water system problems. Federal agencies aimed at farmers were made aware of the problems of rural residents generally, including the special problems of small, isolated, but still non-farm rural communities. In addition, at the state level, legislative and funding distribution changes brought about by DWP and VWP have made better water services available to communities.

The link between water and poverty may not be immediately obvious, but TAP saw a connection and attempted to solve the poverty problem in yet another unorthodox way. The concept of poverty as a combination of life conditions—rather than as a single problem, lack of money—meant that TAP could take money allocated for helping the poor and use it to provide what is essentially a community service to low-income rural residents. Indirectly, TAP's wide-angle view of the poverty problem has helped impoverished rural areas around the country. The growth of the Demonstration Water Project and the development of National Demonstration Water Project brought potable water to homes far removed from the Roanoke Valley. TAP has always had the vision to see that poverty is not a simple condition, and that the problems of poverty are not simply solved.

7

TOWARD A
NEW DECLARATION

The Long Truce

THE EARLY YEARS were the glory years. Sargent Shriver provided imaginative leadership to the Office of Economic Opportunity, and he filled the agency with some of the brightest and most committed people in the country. Community action agencies like TAP and state equal opportunity offices were established throughout the country. For the first time, the poor of America had champions at local, state, and national levels. Needy people were fed, housed, trained, and cared for medically. They were involved in decision making and represented in court. Their children knew the joy of working in school and playing in neighborhoods.

In 1965, it seemed to American liberals that the forces of economic justice had triumphed once and for all. Conservative critics of the war on poverty continued to claim that masses of money were being thrown at a problem that could not be solved. And they trumpeted every finding of fraud or corruption in the poverty program—some of which were true—as proof of federal failure. But the trouncing of the arch conservative Barry Goldwater in the presidential election of 1964 appeared to have delivered a permanently crippling blow to the American right wing. The Great Society lay just around the corner.

It was not to be. For just around the corner lay the Vietnam War, and the attention that had been focused on poverty shifted to Southeast Asia. By 1966, the national mood had changed. The same voters who had been horrified by shoeless children in Appalachia now saw people shot to death on TV. In addition to fighting poverty, the Johnson administration was fighting falling dominoes, and the escalation of the second war led to a truce in the first. It was to be another 15 years, however, before the official end of the war on poverty was signaled by the closing of its national headquarters.

In the final analysis, the guns of Vietnam outweighed any domestic issues. The poor people of America became secondary to the problems of Southeast Asia. The same Democratic constituency that endorsed poverty programs demonstrated violently against the war. When Hubert Humphrey, a great poverty warrior, ran for president in 1968, he was hobbled by Vietnam and ultimately, though narrowly, rejected by the electorate in favor of Richard Nixon. Two wars were one too many for the voters.

In the last years of the Johnson administration, community action had suffered only from neglect. When Richard Nixon came to the Oval Office, there was active hostility. While he expressed the standard concern for the needy, an attack on OEO was launched under traditional conservative headings: returning responsibilities to the states, eliminating fraud and abuse, reducing federal spending. Almost before OEO reached its full strength, its power began to erode.

Some federal agencies complained that the OEO was administering programs that more reasonably belonged to them. For example, Job Corps and employment training programs seemed more fittingly carried out by the Department of Labor, and Head Start and health care seemed the province of the Department of Health, Education, and Welfare. OEO was gradually transformed into a "catalyst" agency, losing many of the operating programs that gave it a strong local constituency. The agency quickly was robbed of its elan and sense of mission, to say nothing of its political clout, and loomed as a lamb for slaughter when Nixon was reelected in 1972.

The chosen slaughter instrument was Howard Phillips, then and now a right-wing ideologue, who was appointed acting director of OEO. Fearful of congressional rejection, Nixon never sent the nomination to the Hill. Instead, he armed Phillips with the "acting" title and gave him a mandate to dismantle OEO and the community action program.

Community action agencies turned from assisting the poor to fighting for their institutional lives. (Much of the Phillips period is filed at TAP in folders marked "survival.") Phillips divested OEO of programs, blocked new ones, and fostered the agency's slide into atrophy. Many staff people were laid off and an attempt was made to eliminate community action entirely. The CAP world fought back with pickets and with protests to the Congress, which retained an interest in the issue and blocked Phillips as often as possible.

In the end, it was not so much Phillips's callous hatchet work on community action that brought him down as Nixon's spurning of the Congress.

In response to a suit against Phillips by three interested organizations, a federal court found that "...the acts or omissions or both, including all rules, regulations guidelines, instructions, and other communications, written or oral, heretofore published, promulgated or otherwise communicated, directing, providing for, or intended to accomplish the termination, dissolution, or abolition of the Office of Economic Opportunity, or of the termination of funding or functioning of Community Action Agencies... are unauthorized by law, illegal, and in excess of statutory authority." In other words, Phillips had been acting illegally. Although his title was acting director, Phillips never had his name submitted to Congress; his candidacy for the position was never considered. Both Phillips and Nixon—for different reasons—were forced to leave office.

Howard Phillips may have lost the battle but he won the

war. OEO's image was now irretrievably tarnished, and in late 1974, Congress created a new agency, the Community Services Administration, in its place. The alternative, favored by President Ford, was to transfer all OEO functions to HEW, a move opposed strongly by the community action people. CSA was left with the community action program, a host of economic development corporations, some special projects, and no credibility.

Not surprisingly, many able and dedicated people left for greener pastures, and CSA fell heir to the drones and time servers in the federal bureaucracy. At one time, it was said, the subtraction of five people from CSA would have left it with no brains whatsoever. Black humor replaced the up-and-at-'em slogans while agency graffiti and internal turf squabbles became the primary concerns of poverty "warriors."

Unfortunately, the disarray at the bottom in CSA was matched by a vacuum at the top. The last respectable director of the agency was Alvin J. Arnett, who succeeded Phillips. Arnett worked on the mistaken presumption that his job was to breath life into CSA. He set about giving support to new program initiatives and building support with local CAAs and state agencies. This was not what the administration had in mind. The story is that one day after lunch, Arnett was called to the White House by presidential assistant Dean Burch, and was told to have his desk cleaned out by close of business. Arnett was followed by a succession of somnolent nonentities. (Secretaries reported that one director spent most of his time sleeping at his desk.)

The return of the Democrats to the White House in 1976 did nothing to arrest the decline of community action at the national level. President Carter was full of kind words for the poor but no money for programs, and CSA leadership hit a new low. Carter's choice was a political twofer, Graciela Olivarez, who achieved the dubious distinction of alienating both the White House *and* the Congress in her tenure.

By the time President Reagan was elected, CSA had sunk to such depths in public esteem that not even diehard liberals mourned its passing, which came in 1981 as one of the first acts of the Reagan administration. The last days of the agency typified what it had become—employees fought to protect their seniority rights while the remains of the community action program were transferred to the Department of Health and Human Services. For 15 years, a truce had been called on the poverty war; and now it was officially over.

Actually, the Reagan administration wanted, in effect, to abolish the community action program, as well as CSA, by lumping it into a "social services block grant" to be controlled by the states. Congress did resist this, and the result was a separate "community services block grant" so that local CAAs at least had a protected funding source. Funding, however, has been substantially reduced, and the desire to terminate the program itself has not abated. (For example, in 1984 appropriations, the administration again proposed the elimination of the community action program while making its activities eligible for support under the social services block grant now in place. But the latter would be increased only $50 million to accommodate $350 million worth of activities under the separate block grant.) It is clear that community action programs are slowly being maneuvered into oblivion—at least that is the intention of the conservatives who control the White House.

The Institutional Legacy

The war on poverty was intended to bring institutional change, to destigmatize poverty in the eyes of officialdom, to affect for the better the way poor people are treated. From this vantage point, the record thus far is one of success.

To begin with, the war on poverty resulted in the training of large numbers of minorities, who then entered the work force. The antipoverty programs gave thousands of minority workers a chance to work in jobs that had previously been closed to them. The number of black, Hispanic, and women administrators who got their start in OEO programs is enormous; for many people, working for the war on poverty was a direct road out of their own disadvantaged state. The examples range from the former welfare mother who is now a teacher to the potential dropout who became interested in sports and went to college. There are many big city mayors today—including the mayor of the nation's capital—who began their careers as poverty warriors.

In addition, many of the programs that were initiated by the war on poverty have at least found grudging acceptance. Head Start programs continue to provide stimulation for preschoolers; health care clinics and service organizations provide medical treatment to the indigent; Medicaid would not exist without the war on poverty; food stamps feed the hungry; fuel assistance helps to heat low-income households. Though these programs may be administered by Agriculture, HHS, Commerce, or other departments, they are all a part of the OEO/CSA legacy.

The most effective part of the institutional legacy may be the community action agency network itself. Some CAAs have been absorbed by local governments, but many hundreds remain functioning as the independent entities they set out to be. They are still serving as foci for community self-help efforts. They are still running day-care centers, clinics, and athletic events. They are still helping minorities and the poor get a start in life. And federal money is still available to them, though as block grants through the state. CAAs must compete with other programs for state government funds, and many also have had success soliciting private corporations and other nonfederal sources. The CAAs are still on the front lines of the war on poverty, though on a skirmish level.

Another kind of change concerns attitudes toward poverty, which have changed for the better. The poor are now seen as people with rights that may be enforced, rather than as charity cases deserving occasional handouts. Reforms begun under OEO have had long-term effects on local welfare departments and community health policies. Disadvantaged people are more likely to be treated with respect now.

Prior to 1981, these gains seemed assured, and those of an optimistic mind were apt to pronounce them a permanent part of the American scene. Although poverty had not been totally bested, mused those of liberal bent, its demise was only a matter of time, because all the appropriate institutions and attitudes were in place. The Force, in other words, was with us.

The election of Ronald Reagan has forced a reassessment of all these assumptions. Whatever Reagan's own nature—and he is widely perceived as an affable man—there is no question that the people empowered by his election or emboldened by his rhetoric do not have a vision of a Great Society or a New Frontier or a Fair Deal or a New Deal or any of the social utopias that have inspired America's policy makers for the last half century. The New Right is literally and figuratively in the saddle, and the voices of liberalism that cheered the war on poverty have receded to a whisper.

The Reagan grin cannot mask the fact that America is in danger of entering a dark age in terms of social progress. It is not just that social program spending has shrunk to a trickle. After all, the federal budget process has always been characterized by boom and bust as far as the poor are concerned. Changing attitudes are the real cause for concern as they lead America to a complete and dangerous institutional reorientation.

The trickle-down theory has been solidly enthroned as the new prescription for social betterment. Present policies—

whether tax laws or deregulation of banks and businesses or inaction in the face of unemployment—are all based on the premise that the nurturing of the rich will lead to the nourishment of the poor, despite substantial historical evidence to the contrary. The belief that problems should be attacked at the source—a notion now derided as passe even at gatherings of wine-and-cheese liberals—has been replaced by worship at the altar of the Market.

And these days, when the federal government does intervene, it is apt to be on the wrong side. The Justice Department, long a champion of the rights of minorities, now files its amicus briefs with those who would discriminate. The Legal Services Corporation, which usually provided the only court assistance available for the poor, is being hounded out of existence. The New Right's idea of a good law is one that forces birth control clinics to squeal on their teenage clients, or school districts to turn away the children of aliens, or women to seek illegal abortions. "Means tests" as the price for economic assistance are much in vogue, and food stamp fraud is prosecuted more vigorously than murder.

Thus, it is premature to count the blessings of the institutional legacy left by the war on poverty. The poverty warriors have taken the high ground, but they are hard put to hold it against the forces of Reaganism. For 50 years a guerrilla army, these Market Militias have now become the regulars in the battle for the American myth.

The Persistence of Poverty

As enunciated by the New Right (which is different from the Old Right only in that the apostles are younger), the American myth is as follows: The United States was founded on laissez-faire economic, social, and political principles, which allowed the virtuous and hard working to prevail; and so the land was developed, and America became a Great

Nation. All (except for a few malcontents and ne'er-do-wells) were happy and prosperous until the federal government began to intervene, hamstringing the industrious entrepreneurs with regulations and taxing their profits in order to waste money on the undeserving poor. The market was thus prevented from bestowing its benefits, and inflation threatened to impoverish everyone. Luckily, Ronald Reagan arrived to reinstitute the "principles that made America great"; and soon, very soon, as benefits trickle down to even the lowliest among us, all will be well again.

It is all bosh. Laissez-faire principles may have served us well when America was a fledgling agrarian society with a continent to be settled and seemingly inexhaustible resources to be exploited. But even then, there were substantial imperfections in the idyllic picture, such as the millions of Americans who were held in slavery because they were black, slaughtered or dispossessed because they were red, or excluded from the rights of citizenship because they were yellow. Countless others of all races were held in peonage or indentured status because they were poor.

With the coming of the Industrial Revolution, even more blights appeared. The laissez-faire system allowed great fortunes to be built, and enough of this trickled down to create a substantial middle class. But the social cost, to say nothing of the environmental cost, was staggering—child labor, sweatshops, poorhouses, slums, bread lines, and black lung. And the laissez-faire system did nothing to eliminate the pervasive racial discrimination, de facto and de jure, that condemned the colored (black, red, brown, or yellow) quarter of the population to perpetual poverty.

The fact is that the supposedly impersonal market could be rigged—and it was. Exploitative practices were used to gain corporate power, and corporate power was then used to further disadvantage those who lacked it. As John Kenneth Galbraith pointed out long ago, the exploitative tendencies of American capitalism were never checked by competition on the same side of the market. Such checks as have existed have come from across the market, sometimes through self-help efforts (for example, unions, cooperatives) but also through, or in combination with, government power; people began using their numbers to gain politically what they could not achieve economically.

In reality, then, American history has had two faces. For many, it has indeed been a land of opportunity where people with skill, determination, and luck could get ahead, assuming they were in a favored market position to begin with or could successfully manipulate market forces. Rags to riches. For others, it has been a land of disenchantment where no amount of individual effort could overcome a disadvantaged market position. Rags to rags. The same system, the same conditions, that created opportunity also created poverty.

In a sense, America has been forced to fight a war on poverty from the very beginning of its history. That is, we have used the power of government to alleviate the poverty either ignored or created by the market system. The free schools were created for poor children. The Homestead Act was poverty legislation. The reformers of the late nineteenth century like Jane Addams, Upton Sinclair, and Henry George continued this tradition. Thus, Franklin Roosevelt and Lyndon Johnson were hardly departing from American principles; they were simply mounting a more concerted effort against an age-old problem.

And despite the rear-guard actions of those who seek eternal privileges for the haves—Reagan is the latest to assume power—the war is being won. It is hard to quantify the poverty population in the nineteenth century because there was no official poverty line. Many poor people were hidden on farms, and some groups, such as slaves, were often ignored altogether. But in the days of the robber barons, before the Populist Revolt and the urban reformers, probably one-half to two-thirds of the population was poor. By

1933, the number had declined, as Franklin Roosevelt saw one-third of a nation ill-housed and ill-fed. When Lyndon Johnson launched the first *declared* war on poverty, the usual dimensions of the "other America" were cited at 25 percent of the population. Since then, poverty has been officially defined, and figures have been scrupulously kept, although not so scrupulously interpreted. In 1973, about the time Nixon began to dismantle OEO, the official poverty figure dipped to its lowest point in American history, just over 11 percent.

Since 1973, the poverty figure has increased again, sharply in recent years. It now stands at 15 percent. Since the onset of the Reagan administration, there have been sharp poverty increases; about 35 million Americans are now classified as poor. This is the largest number of poor people we have ever had in American history. The American *poverty population* is substantially greater than *the total population* of Canada. In fact, it is larger than the population of 100 other individual countries.

What can we conclude from this brief tour of American history and America's poverty population? Firstly, poverty has been a persistent fact, not a temporary side effect of depressions or recessions. Secondly, although recent increases in the poor population are cause for concern, the percentage of poor people in our society has moved steadily downward. Thirdly, given overall population increases, the number of poor people is still very large, the largest in our history.

And why has poverty declined, at least in percentage terms? It has been because of the opportunities created by the American economic system *combined with* interventionist strategies pursued on behalf of those disadvantaged by the same economic system. If the market system is left to operate alone, there will be an increase in opportunities for some, primarily those already in a favored position, but the poverty population will surge.

That is why the policies of the New Right must be resisted. They would make the rich richer and the poor both poorer and more numerous. Poverty warriors have no reason to hang their heads; they have not failed. The liberal principles that have sustained the fight against poverty are still valid, and their application is still needed.

A Declaration of Interdependence

The poor of America need a new declaration on their own behalf. But we do not need another declaration of war on poverty; that war never ended. Nor do we need the declaration of an alms race, which is what the Reagan administration seems to have in mind with its prattle about the truly needy. Instead we need what might be called a declaration of interdependence. The fact is that opportunity and poverty are interdependent in American society. The same social-political-economic system that permits opportunity tends to create poverty. To enjoy the benefits of the former, we must take action against the latter. It is a continuing struggle.

The early spirit of the antipoverty movement, the spirit that started TAP and the similar social action agencies scattered throughout the country, was energetic, dedicated, and prepared for a quick victory. Poverty could be eliminated in our time, President Johnson claimed. Community action programs set up "temporary" operations designed to be disbanded as soon as poverty was wiped out.

As a consequence, community action programs like TAP were not viewed by the founders, workers, or funders as permanent organizations. Poverty itself was not permanent, and once it was cured, the organization responsible for helping the poor would wither away like Karl Marx's proletarian state. Once the poor had been trained to help themselves, the helpers would be out of business. Unfortunately, the "temporary expedient" approach to poverty is not effective.

143

The various effective and ineffective poverty programs over the years have demonstrated that it is possible to ameliorate the condition of many of the nation's poor through social means. But the causes are more intractable that anyone thought in the beginning; they are rooted in the American economic system.

The United States is essentially a pluralist society in which basic economic and social decisions are made by a complicated mixture of individuals, small autonomous groups, large private corporations, and public bodies of many types and levels of authority. There is little central planning to achieve predetermined results; instead, results are achieved piecemeal. The emphasis is on freedom, not justice, and on equality of opportunity, at least theoretically, not of results. Most Americans seem to like things that way, at least enough of them do to make any basic change unlikely. The American system creates the opportunity for many people to be comfortably middle class, even rich. Millions have taken advantage of that opportunity.

The same system creates poor people. As we know, the haves tend to exploit the have-nots. But even if all deliberate exploitation were eliminated, there still would be a problem. The basic reason is that there is no established method for matching jobs, people with skills to do the jobs, and people who need jobs. Changing economic conditions (for example, urbanization, automation, computerization) displace workers who cannot acquire new skills quickly enough to prevent a slide into poverty. The ranks of this poverty population are swelled by those who make mistakes (for example, offenders) or have bad luck, particularly the mentally and physically ill and the untalented. Poor people then have children who find it hard to rise above their depressed conditions, and the poverty population rises further.

In order to eliminate these dislocations, we would have to guarantee every adult—and force every adult to accept—a job that supports a decent standard of living. That probably cannot be done in a free society; it is not even attempted in American society.

Could we eliminate poverty through a totally planned economy? Theoretically, yes, at least that portion of poverty traceable to economic maladjustments. In practice, we do not know; there are no historical precedents. The socialist economies that have sprouted in this century have not eliminated poverty, although they have arguably broken up the concentrations of wealth at the top and improved the lot of the poor. But every completely socialist economy, such as the Soviet Union or China, has started with such masses of poor people at the bottom that one cannot pass final judgment on the success of their economic methods. It will take another century, assuming no major wars (a big assumption), before we can truly judge the efficacy of the socialist approach. At the present time, certainly, the Soviet economy is not a very good advertisement for the planned economy.

In any case, total economic planning clearly reduces opportunity for everyone, and this is a high price to pay, even for the elimination of poverty. Would poor people in America be willing to give up the chance of joining the ranks of the well-to-do in order to obtain a larger share of the basic necessities? Probably not.

Can we eliminate poverty while preserving opportunity? Based on our experience thus far, the answer would seem to be yes, assuming we recognize the persistent nature of the problem and do not slacken our efforts. The objective is to have everyone in a position to obtain—through effort—a decent standard of living for himself and his family. And this requires stable jobs with decent wages. But creating these jobs involves more than expanding the economy, the favorite remedy of the trickle-down school. If people do not have some basic minimum of food, clothing, shelter, education, and medical care, they will lack the ability or motivation to take advantage of the jobs that are created. And if they must enter the bank-and-corporation-controlled market with no job security, consumer protection laws, or protection against racial and sex discrimination, they can hardly be guaranteed jobs that are either stable or fairly paid.

The government-backed guarantees of the New Deal—such as Social Security, unemployment compensation, union rights, minimum wages, and so on—made a major contribution to the elimination of poverty. The later programs of the official war on poverty—such as Head Start, Medicare, food stamps, and community action—took us another step closer to the goal of a poverty-free society.

We need to protect these gains while going yet another step. In particular, we need improvements in housing, in medical care, and in education. The poverty agenda is still long, but it is not endless. For the first time in our history, we are within reach of an America that practices what it preaches about equal opportunity. There has always been opportunity, but it has never been equal because poverty for some has been a regular byproduct of the opportunity seized by others. We must see the two as interdependent.

Poverty and Community Action

The significance of community action programs changes once we understand the true nature of poverty. The community action agency is not a temporary expedient against a temporary problem. It is instead a social governor on the economic and social system. If the community action structure is dismantled, there will be fewer ladders out of poverty and the number of poor will increase. By helping the poor where possible, and assisting those who are willing to make the climb, the community action agency makes it clear that there are ways to overcome a disadvantaged background. A well-run community action program provides its poor constituents with the most important asset of all—hope.

But why should anyone care about the poor? Certainly they count for little in the economic market or the political market. They vote less, spend less, produce less, and have less social influence. One reason to care is moral. All ethical codes teach that people have an obligation to help the needy. Certainly, this is a key feature of the Judeo-Christian ethic that dominates America. People who enrich themselves at the expense of others, or to the neglect of others, are committing a moral transgression. In our secular society, we do not punish such transgressions, but we are not bound to respect those who commit them.

Unfortunately, American society provides a steady stream of excuses for those who wish to shirk their moral obligations. "Not all the poor are deserving; the programs are full of waste and abuse; the private sector will do the job; I gave at the office." And so on, ad infinitum. There are always excuses for greed.

For those who choose not to act out of altruism, there are plenty of self-interested reasons for trying to eliminate poverty or curtail it as much as possible.

Although a few poor people are a nuisance, a large class of the very poor becomes a political and social danger. When too many people in a society are poor, there is always the danger that they will take power and possessions away from those who have them. A link between poverty and crime is widely recognized, and it is easily understandable that more poor people means more potential criminals.

A large poor population is dangerous in another way as well. When a sizable segment of society is disgruntled and dissatisfied, this segment becomes open to exploitation by politicians of a revolutionary bent. The poor themselves have little power, yet large numbers of them can be organized into a revolutionary force. Any country that allows a large number of citizens to live in poverty and misery is ignoring its own welfare.

Thus, continuing to work against poverty is crucial to the

welfare of, not only the poor, but the rest of society. Community action programs work directly with the poor, providing visible evidence of the government's interest in them. For example, during the summer of 1968, when cities all across America were paralyzed by riots, Roanoke remained cool. A major reason for the lack of civil disturbance was TAP's involvement with the dissatisfied black community. The TAP staff worked directly with black leaders to help them make their complaints heard; the Roanoke ghetto did not erupt into violence in part because its residents felt that someone was listening, that someone was concerned about the grievances felt by blacks.

There are financial incentives for poverty programs, as well. A number of the more effective approaches to poverty are remarkably cost effective. In the case of prisoner programs, for example, a reduction in the recidivism rate eventually saves the state billions of dollars in criminal court, prison construction and maintenance, and correctional costs. Reducing crime saves the state money, and more money, in the long run, than the program costs. The same can be argued for education programs; children who are taught to read effectively early in life will be saved remedial work later and will become more productive adults. Some training programs also generate more than their cost in increased tax revenues from the participants. Thus, the money spent to fight poverty is not pure charity; it is returned to the government in a number of ways from programs that work.

The question can always be raised, "Why community action agencies? Why not some direct government action?" The answer is, if something else works as well, use it. In many cases, community action functions can be taken over by local or municipal governments, which can do just as good a job.

But in many cases, the only alternative to a community action program is no program at all. If the responsibility for poverty assistance were passed to the municipalities, many would simply cease to operate any programs, or operate them in ways that would ignore the real intended beneficiaries. This is not an indictment of local jurisdictions. Many do run programs effectively. But the fact remains that, in most areas, the poor are in the minority. They have less political power, they vote less, and they are less well organized than the middle class.

Yet, almost any city administration will use available funds to sponsor programs that generate votes. And most of those votes are middle class. As a consequence, a local government would be far more likely to use its funds to run, for instance, a program for unemployed middle-class workers than for those lower-class, unskilled workers who may never even have had a regular job.

Another reason for keeping federal control over poverty assistance is financial; local officials, especially if they are governing low-income cities, may not have enough funds to operate any kind of program. A city with a large poor population obviously would have trouble raising a budget large enough to meet its needs.

Finally, there is the issue of fairness. Local government can be appallingly insensitive; the civil rights movement showed just how supportive of the status quo small town government can be. Years of bigotry and adherence to the local system ensure that many towns would, if given poverty funds, continue to ignore those for whom the funds are aimed.

Poverty is really a national problem, anyway. It should be dealt with by the nation in a large and systematic way. Although "styles" of poverty may vary from area to area—for example, the relative proportions of urban to rural poor in any state can vary widely—the problem is really rooted in the American system. And a systemic problem needs a systemic plan of attack. These programs need a substantial national presence and endorsement and oversight from the national government.

The issue of national participation in local affairs is as old as the country itself. James Madison, in the *Federalist Papers,* points out that when a jurisdiction is too small, what is good for the local majority may not be good for the larger national majority. The poor would likely be ill-served by a program run by the wealthier majority in the area. In addition, the use of federal funds ensures an even distribution of benefits. By taking funds from richer cities and giving them to poorer ones, assistance is sent where it is needed.

Another extremely important advantage of working through community action agencies is precisely the absence of governmental administration. A community action program is not the government and, therefore, is more likely to win favor with its clients, who mistrust anything smacking of bureaucracy. People who have been arrested, drafted, or tied up in red tape by the government are going to be wary of any government assistance.

This element of trust is demonstrated quite well by the various studies performed on TAP. Most of the residents in the TAP service area had heard of Total Action Against Poverty, and most of them thought it was helping the community even if they themselves had not received any benefit from it. The government ties to TAP were disguised enough so that it was not perceived by Roanoke residents as invasive or meddling. This lack of government overtones is particularly effective in the ex-offender programs. For many exconvicts, anything that looks like the "system" means trouble. They are experts at conning and manipulation; they manipulate their jailers, and once released, they try to manipulate their parole officers. Correction officials are all thought of as belonging to the system, a system that is to be short-circuited at every step, even if for no reason other than to make things difficult. A community action program does not carry the same stigma.

The "TAP style" of free-wheeling, innovative, casual operation is more effective when dealing with ex-offenders and other mistrustful groups. The programs are more flexible; those who run them are more like peers of the clients; and the overall atmosphere is one of mutual aid rather than bureaucratic assistance. People like Lin Atkins and Betty Desper exemplify the peer aspect of community action; programs are run by those who understand the condition of their target group, not by persons trained in social work but ignorant of the street.

This personnel issue is also an advantage of the community action structure. The government has to standardize, to compartmentalize, to deal evenly with all strata. A community action program can afford to hire those the government could not or would not employ: the undereducated, the inexperienced, the ex-offender. TAP has had great success in taking people with no qualifications other than motivation, intelligence, and interest and turning them into successful program directors.

The government, functioning under restraints as it does, is unable to work innovatively and creatively. A community action program is able to operate in a far more sensitive, sensible, flexible, and humane manner. The community action program is responsive to the needs of its service area in ways that a larger bureaucracy cannot match. Unworkable programs can be dispensed with easily, and more effective ones substituted. The nature of the staff and the scale of the operation tend to make the process of assistance friendlier, like a neighbor helping out in an emergency rather than like a social worker giving advice. Federal financial resources are needed, but community action gives a freedom unknown to larger programs.

Total Action Against Poverty shows what can be done in a community action environment. It is not a typical community action program; it has been far more innovative, responsive, and creative than most. It has had its failures, but it also has had enormous success in many areas, helping to improve the quality of life for thousands of Roanoke

Valley residents. TAP's effect on its service area has been large; TAP programs have touched the lives of many.

But there are still poor people in Roanoke, still under-privileged, uneducated, unmotivated, handicapped, or unemployable residents in the valley. Even though TAP has helped many people, there are many more who need assistance. The idea of giving a "quick fix" to the system is unrealistic. Instead, community action programs in Roanoke and across the country must be a permanent part of each community, permanently funded, permanently ready to deal with social problems on a local level. Maintaining this resource is a federal responsibility.

From the very beginning of the war on poverty, community action agencies have had to fight for funds. No sooner were programs like TAP set up and funded than they were trimmed and cut back. The constant struggle for grants and funding weakens the administration of any organization, and a community action program is no exception. If funding were more secure, if some degree of continuity could be built into the system, agencies could devote more of their energy and efforts to preparing and administering effective programs. What good is designing a program and then having it cut away from the bottom, sometimes even before it can be fairly evaluated? The community action program should be seen by the government as a permanent part of the superstructure, an individual entity that, though funded by the government, works privately in the public interest.

It has been a central tenet of American liberalism in the twentieth century that the power of the central government should be used to support those who are disadvantaged by the market economy. Richard Nixon and Jimmy Carter brought this tenet into disrepute, Nixon by proving that the federal government could be venal and corrupt, Carter by demonstrating that it could be bungling and inefficient.

As American liberals have gone into hiding, the New Right has poured into the void, attempting to undo 50 years of work for equal opportunity and reclaim federal power for the use of privileged interests. It is a time of danger for the underprivileged people, who had liberalism as their champion.

Even more dangerous are the now-fashionable neo-liberals. They profess great concern for poor people but have lost all taste for social battle and all hope of victory. They retreat instead into voguish nostrums with conservative appeal such as "public-private partnerships" and "industrial policy."

If American prosperity is not to be washed away in another tide of poverty, true liberalism must reassert itself. Liberals must come out of the closet and say: "We made some mistakes, particularly in our choice of leaders, but we were right and we were winning; we intend to win again. We will eliminate poverty and discrimination. And we will not bankrupt the country because we will ensure that those who are able to pay for these things do so. We will not let private greed override the public interest, and we will not allow our economy to become the captive of corporate power."

When there is a national leader willing to make this speech—and mean it—the war on poverty can finally be won. It is not lack of resources that has frustrated us but lack of commitment; it is not our methodology that is flawed but our leadership. Now is the time to right our course and fulfill the promise of American society for all our people.

EPILOGUE

The world will little note nor long remember what we say here, but it can never forget what they did here.

Abraham Lincoln, the Gettysburg Address

IT IS 7:30 P.M., September 22, 1983. The cool of the night air does not go unnoticed by Roanoke Valley residents after a record-breaking summer heat wave.

It is the time of the September meeting of the Virginia Association of Community Action Agencies (VACAA). Many still remember it as the association Bristow built. In the first years of the war on poverty in Virginia, Bristow brought the community action executive directors together to form the association, telling them that "our strength is in working together and supporting each other." This evening, over 300 community action people from 28 community action agencies, the Virginia Water Project, the Virginia CARES network, and the Virginia Housing Coalition are gathered under the elegant high ceilings and chandeliers of the Hotel Roanoke ballroom. This is the banquet that concludes three hectic days of committee meetings, training sessions, and board meetings.

There is deep significance in the meeting place. The Hotel Roanoke dominates a rise of land at the northern entrance to the city and looks down across the railroad tracks to the heart of Roanoke's rejuvenated financial and commercial district. It is an elegant structure whose brown-on-white half-timbered Tudor chalet exterior is complemented by the sloping green lawns that flow like the skirts of an evening gown. Modeled after the old station house hotels of England, the

Hotel Roanoke was built and is owned by the Norfolk and Western Railroad, which continues to be the underpinning of the Roanoke economy. The black uniforms and white aprons of an all-black dining room serving staff are a reminder, not only of Deep South hospitality and elegance, but of antebellum and post-Reconstruction times when blacks could serve but not be served. Always included in any of the listings of great old hotels in America, the Hotel Roanoke is the visiting place of presidential candidates, governors, and other visiting dignitaries.

The significance was not lost on the honorable mayor, Dr. Noel C. Taylor, who had addressed more than 1,000 black masons at their annual meeting the night before. Dr. Taylor, now in his third term as mayor, remembers aloud the time in 1961 when he came to Roanoke as the pastor of the High Street Baptist Church, situated down the street from the hotel. "It is not that long ago, and we can still remember it, that neither I nor any of you could enter this hotel, the symbol of Roanoke society and establishment, and get a room to sleep in or food to quench our hunger nor water to quench our thirst." The significance of this night is not lost on Herb Guerrant, who for 14 years has been the executive director of the Fauquier Community Action Agency and vice-president of the Virginia Water Project. He was a waiter at the Hotel Roanoke before the civil rights public accommodations laws went into effect. Bristow had hired him as a supervisor in TAP's early neighborhood development efforts. Nor is it lost on Sara Holland, TAP youth director and vice-president of the Roanoke NAACP, who, with her husband, was active in integration efforts. Nor on Martha Ogden, director of Community Outreach, who was one of the grassroots neighborhood residents that joined with Cabell Brand to start TAP. Nor on Alvin Nash, director of the TAP Southwest Virginia Foodbank, whose uncle, the Reverend Tom Cruz, was a beloved social activist in his church, on the TAP staff, and on the Senior Citizens

Advisory Council. Nor on any person in the banquet hall.

This is not the first time that TAP has used the hotel facilities. There were two other notable situations over a decade ago. At the beginning of the 1970s, Cabell and Bristow invited all of the local public officials of the Roanoke Valley to hear the regional director of the Office of Economic Opportunity. During the luncheon, and as the director was speaking, Bristow fell asleep at the head table. While he snoozed, his elbow slid precariously close to a water pitcher at the edge of the table, creating a sense of high drama for the spellbound audience. Later, the director commented on the unusual attentiveness and apparent interest of those who had attended.

At the second event, Cabell and the TAP staff had hosted a seminar on poverty for 100 members of the prestigious Young Presidents' Organization, of which Cabell was a member. Three days of meetings included a specially designed poverty game simulation, a drama on poverty written by Tom Atkins, a drama professor at Hollins College, and a luncheon that matched businessmen with welfare recipients hired as experts on poverty. For many of the Young Presidents, that meeting had a profound impact.

On this evening in September, the banquet room begins to fill with dinner guests. Entertainer James Wise is at the piano singing "Always on My Mind." On the previous evening, his group, James Wise and Company, appeared at the Virginia CARES "Blue Jeans Ball" benefit held in the hotel's Shenandoah Room. The dance, cosponsored by WTOY, the local black radio station, raised over $1,000 for reentry funds for prisoners returning to the community.

The Reverend Ely Ogden, the board member from the Delaney Court Civic League in Roanoke County, gives the invocation. He has as his guest Dr. Harry Nickens, member of the Roanoke County Board of Supervisors, who will be honored for arranging the donation of 250 gallons of paint to the low-income residents of Delaney Court.

As dinner guests queue up on either side of the buffet tables, familiar faces appear. Georgia Meadows, now in her ninth year as a TAP board member, is present. She is the president of the area's League of Older Americans board of directors and a senator to Virginia's Silver-Haired Legislature. She has survived both the death of her beloved husband and a long illness this year and regained her strength. She has just returned from Indiana where she was the keynote speaker for the 10,000 delegates of the Lott Carie Foreign Mission Convention. She is also serving her term as the president of the Women's Education and Missionary Convention to the Virginia Baptist State Convention. This year, she will be honored by the *Roanoke & Times World-News* as one of the five outstanding women of the year in southwest Virginia.

Retired now, Betty Desper was also elected to Virginia's Silver-Haired Legislature and continues to serve as a consultant to TAP's housing program. This year, the housing component, under the leadership of B. B. Bagby, will complete its 2000th weatherized home and its 56th housing rehabilitation project. The TAP board has set aside a revolving loan fund for the total rehabilitation of dilapidated housing. The first house is completed and on the market.

Wilma Warren continued in her sixth year as the executive director of the Virginia Water Project. Virginia Water Project, the demonstration project begun by TAP in 1969, is today a full partner in the Virginia rural water and wastewater delivery system, and its Southeast Rural Community Assistance Project (SE/R-CAP) is increasingly regarded as a necessary resource to the state and local governments in Delaware, Maryland, North Carolina, South Carolina, Georgia, and Florida. Over 22,000 low-income Virginians have safe drinking water or sanitary waste facilities as a direct result of VWP and local community action agencies such as TAP. When local projects under development in the six other states are completed, 12,600

157

additional low-income people will have these vital services. VWP's Private/Public Partnerships project is bringing the private sector into the development process, and during the past year, over $82,000 in cash, materials, and labor has been contributed.

Lin Atkins has been executive director of the Virginia CARES project since its formation in 1979. The prerelease/postrelease program of Virginia CARES has aided 5,000 Virginia inmates and ex-offenders as they have left prison and returned to their communities. The program has received a transition grant from the Ford Foundation and praise from a study by the National Institute of Corrections. Cabell Brand has championed the program with Governor Charles Robb and has asked the Virginia General Assembly for $2 million a year to fully implement the program, which could save the commonwealth more than $10 million by reducing the need for more prisons. In the last month, Virginia CARES, along with the community agencies of southwest Virginia, has been awarded a grant to deter non-violent convicted felons from prison through a Community Diversion Incentive program grant awarded by the Virginia Department of Corrections.

Jayne Thomas is completing her first year as director of the new Office of Community Action in the Virginia Department of Social Services. It was she who created the office with the drafting of the first Neighborhood Assistance Act and the Community Action Act, which were subsequently enacted into law. The first allows businesses and individuals a 50 percent tax credit for donations to approved community action projects. The second provides for the continuation of community action agencies using a state mechanism for administering federal funds for community action. In addition to restoring the $600,000 that was cut from the Virginia federal allocation and working with agencies to develop the least bureaucratic reporting systems, Jayne is producing a filmed Virginia community action annual report entitled *The Forgotten War*. She is also completing a statewide economic impact statement, modeled after TAP's, that documents that community action in the Commonwealth of Virginia for 1982-83 had an economic impact of $70 million and a saving to the public of $20 million.

Ted Edlich is nearing his ninth year as TAP's executive director. The agency, faced with a loss of a quarter million dollars of funds, has been streamlined administratively; yet every program emphasis of the past has been preserved while many new ones have been added. In spite of staff upheavals surrounding administrative cuts and subsequent unionization efforts, Ted has weathered the storm and relentlessly pressed for new program development and taken advantage of every conceivable financial opportunity. Recently, on behalf of the weatherization program, he convinced the Virginia State Welfare Board to contribute an additional three million dollars to the Virginia weatherization effort.

Congressman James Olin, the first Democrat from the Sixth Congressional District to be elected in three decades, is the guest speaker for the evening. Also on hand are Senator Ray Garland, renowned for his oratory, and Democratic Delegate "Chip" Woodrum, the author of the Virginia Community Action Act of 1981.

There are other community action leaders as well: Alvin Nash, who has built the Southwest Virginia Foodbank to where it distributes 150,000 pounds of food a month to 800 people through its 214 member organizations; Sara Holland, whose youth education and employment programs serve over 2,000 young people a year; Ann Poskocil, whose three-year efforts have just resulted in the funding of Project Discovery by the Department of Education. Project Discovery will help 600 minority children adequately prepare for college entrance and a college education, a project destined for replication; Bernice Wade, who has expanded TAP's employment and training program to include adult education, clerical skills training, and classes in construction skills; Martha Ogden,

159

whose staff each year provides organizing assistance to 25 community groups and emergency aid to over 2000 individuals in the TAP territory; Bob Campbell, who, not only works with ex-offenders and battered women, but who now runs the local VASAP education programs for people caught driving under the influence and a VISTA-funded project that works with the alcohol problems of young people who are in trouble with the courts; Cleo Sims, who has expanded the relatively flush Head Start program, the only program to receive monetary increases, to include three additional centers serving over 500 preschool children; Ben Bray, whose training expertise has affected 80 percent of the people in the room from all over Virginia; Nancy Harper, finance director, who guards the till and ensures question-free audits; Gail Mayhew, whose personnel duties have enabled TAP to continue full medical and dental benefits for its employees. If ever mere mortals could replicate the miracle of the fishes and loaves, these people have.

Conspicuously absent is Cabell Brand. Cabell approaches his 20th year as the distinguished president of the TAP board. In an award ceremony sponsored by the Friends of VISTA in June of 1980, Cabell was selected as the businessman in the United States who had contributed the most to the war on poverty. Of him, Sargent Shriver said, "Cabell, if we had three businessmen like you, we could change this country and win the poverty war." Cabell has increased the hours he contributes to community action lobbying at state and federal levels. There is no more articulate spokesman in America. In addition, Cabell has been affecting business leaders and public officials through his involvement in groups such as the Woodlands Conference, in Texas, and the Futures Advisory Board of the Congressional Clearinghouse on the Future, in Washington, D.C. At the time of the meeting, he is touring Indonesia, assessing problems and solutions. He is the best example of his own motto: "Think globally and work locally."

The room quiets to a hush as Councilwoman and former Vice-Mayor Elizabeth Bowles welcomes the conferees on behalf of the city of Roanoke. In a surprise gesture, she honors Sherman Saunders, VACAA president and executive director of the Pittsylvania Community Action Agency, for his leadership which has bound the organization effectively together through the divisive transition from direct federal funding to the state-administered block grant system. Councilwoman Bowles asks Mr. Saunders to stand and places around his neck the key to the city of Roanoke. The group immediately rises; the applause is deafening. Tears come to the president's eyes as he expresses his gratitude. No one is unmoved.

The audience is seated as a distinguished black woman adjusts her glasses and makes her way to the podium. Although her 80 years have not slowed her, her knees are giving her a little trouble this evening. She is dressed in a handsome dark suit, and her shoulders are draped in the finest of fur stoles. She is well known to everyone in the audience.

The woman is Mrs. Hazel Thompson, treasurer of the TAP board. She is a teacher by profession. She can remember when she had to be sent to Virginia State College in Petersburg in 1921 to finish high school because there was no high-school education in Roanoke for black children. She can remember when, as a teacher in the Roanoke city school system, she went to the superintendent of schools and successfully demanded that black and white teachers be seated together and stated that it was an insult to seat black teachers apart in the balcony of the auditorium. "Butch" Thompson, as she was called, rarely turned down a righteous cause and rarely lost. She taught for 47 years in the Roanoke city schools before retirement, a total of three generations and over 4,000 children. Everything she touches seems to grow—children, plants, animals, and causes. She has the touch of life.

In Roanoke, she is known as Mrs. Harrison School. It was her group, the Northwest Improvement Association, whose members dreamed of the day when the Harrison School, the first black high school in southwest Virginia, built in 1918, could be restored to community use.

The Harrison School, a three-story, red brick building, solidly stands facing Harrison Street, its handsome, graceful exterior marred only by a leaky roof, broken windows, padlocked doors, and an asphalt yard punctuated with weeds. It was a fragile dream that, to all but the TAP staff and board, seemed an impossible one. The costs of the project ranged from $500,000 to a million dollars. There were no expanding programs to house in the school to defray costs of construction and maintenance. TAP had no experience in renovating anything beyond a frame-structured single-family dwelling. The City Planning Department and the Roanoke Housing Authority thought the program unlikely. The Virginia Historical Society would not even consider recognizing the building; it was too new. All there was was a dilapidated school of little value, one-time "separate but equal" facilities that were no longer needed, a group of elderly citizens, and a nearly 80-year-old black woman with sparkling eyes and a determined jaw. Oh, yes, and a community action agency whose funding was threatened.

For those who had eyes to see, the project had three grand things to commend it. First, it was a symbol of a deteriorating northwest community, the largest remaining community of black residents in the city of Roanoke and the oldest section of the city. If something could be done to turn it around, perhaps it would inspire the entire area with hope and energy. Second, it had Hazel Thompson, the most charismatic, persistent, sophisticated, eloquent neighborhood leader in the city. Until now, a light hidden under a bushel. Third, it was impossible! Nothing excites Ted Edlich and his staff more than something impossible. It is the way of community action people.

Over a three-year period, Hazel Thompson led the effort. When a Neighborhood Assistance Grant was turned down by HUD, she and the TAP staff met with HUD officials to determine the problems. She met with the president of the First Federal Savings and Loan to get a $250,000 loan commitment. She and her organization attended hearings for the spending of local Community Development Block Grant money and encouraged the city to set aside $150,000 toward the project. When the HUD grant was funded, a feat in itself, she chaired a local fund-raising effort that brought in another $20,000. Month after month, her group held rummage and bake sales that added a dollar here and a dollar there. Hazel and her colleagues met with Republican congressman Caldwell Butler, who likewise fell under her spell and secured 13, then 15 more Section Eight housing subsidy commitments, which would over years pay back the initial investment to restore the school.

When the Virginia Historical Society balked at a historical designation, she got the entire Roanoke state legislative delegation to back Delegate Vic Thomas's bill to legislate the Harrison School a historic landmark. They got the Virginia Historical Society moving, and now the school is on both the Virginia and national registers. When extensions on the HUD grant and the Section Eight allotments ran out, she persuaded the director of the Virginia HUD Office, Margaret White, to grant an extension in spite of pressure by the national office to return the funds. Hazel walked the alleyway behind the school and got permission to block the alley and acquired critical parcels of land from residents. She attended meeting with architects and developers and negotiated the arrangement with local developers.

Sometime around April 1984, the Harrison School will be remodeled into 28 apartments for the elderly and handicapped; it will also have the Harrison School Hazel Thompson History and Cultural Center—a place that will honor the history and the cultural achievements of the black population in Roanoke. Even now, Hazel has been continuing to meet with Senator Tribble of Virginia to urge him to pass special legislation through the U.S. Congress so that the historical and cultural center can be exempt from IRS legislation that has prohibited its expansion to the total space previously planned for it.

The room is quiet. Mrs. Thompson is ready to speak.

Master of Ceremonies, platform guests, visiting VACAA members, ladies and gentlemen: It is an honor and privilege to welcome you. I am a member of the board of Total Action Against Poverty, founded by Mr. Cabell Brand, a businessman who cares about people and has continued to care and work for them and with them. . . . All of us in this room have much in common. We are all working to make this world a better place—to help children get a head start in life, young men and women improve their health and homes, and even help those who have made mistakes in their lives and are willing to start again.

We welcome you because you are angels in disguise, who bring food, clothing, shelter, health, kindness, and joy to others who are unable to do it all themselves.

We challenge you to continue in your good work. . . .

Somewhere an angel of another sort, and yet the same sort, a red-bearded angel, prone to sailing celestial boats in the heavenly clouds, an angel known as Bristow, is surely saying, "Right on!"

INDEX

Abernathy, Ralph, 39
abortions, 139
Acapulco, bullfight in, 38
Addams, Jane, 141
adult education, 26, 159; see also education
after-school care, 25, 95, 96
Aid to the Elderly, 101
Alabama, 19
alcohol and drug abuse programs, of TAP, 59-60, 87
alcohol problems, of youth, 160
Alcohol Services of TAP, 87
alcohol-counseling services, TAP spinoff program, 53
Alcoholic Detoxification Center, 83
Alcoholics Anonymous, and HELP, 60
aliens, 74, 139
Alleghany County, pulpwood in, 24
Alleghany County Court Project, CETA staffed, 70
Alternative Education program, 100
America, ex-offender population in, 105
Americans, use of water by, 120
American Correctional Association, funded WINGS, 112
Appalachian coal miners, 15
Arnett, Alvin, 135
art, women in, 88
art classes, for young people, 101, 102
Artemis, women in arts program, 88
Assertiveness Training, 87
Atkins, Lin, 104-05, 112, 118, 151, 156, 158
auto mechanics, NYC graduates trained in, 66
auto mechanics, OIC job, 73
automation, displaces workers, 144
Ayers, Jim, 112

Bagby, B. B., 157
bank deregulation, and poverty, 139

barbering, NYC graduates trained in, 66
Barbour, Nancy, 10
Barone, Sam, 35
Barry, Marion, 137
baseball teams, TAP-organized youth program, 102
basketball, TAP-organized youth program, 102
battered women, 54, 100; see also women
Berlin Blockade of 1948, 30
Bethany House, for women alcoholics, 60
bicycle pump, 5
Big Lick, 22
birth control clinics, 60-61, 139; see also family planning
black, church, 29; community, 45-47; ex-offender, 114; leadership and TAP, 148; OEO administrators, 137; poverty among, 16; power, 19, 28; women, 86; youth, 48
black lung, 140
Black Lung Outreach, 70
blacks, 63-64
Blacksburg, Va., 76
Bland Correctional Center, 113
blood bank donation, 46-47
blue collar work, Industry Bound, 97
Botetourt, Lord, 43
Botetourt, resources of, 24
Botetourt Correctional Unit #25, 110
Botetourt County, part of TAP service area, 42
Botetourt Improvement Association, 43
Bowles, Elizabeth, 161
Brambleton Junior Women's Club, 87
Brand, Cabell, background of, 4, 9-10; as businessman, 160; founder of TAP, 155-56; history of, 30-34; on prisoner's transition shock, 106; and Salem, 51; and Virginia CARES, 158

Brand Shoe Company, 31
Bray, Ben, 160
bread lines, 140
brick laying, OIC job, 73
Bridgewater, Va., 129
Buchanan, Va., 41
budgeting, taught by TAP, 83
Buena Vista Housing Development Corporation, 85
bullfight, 38
Burch, Dean, 135
business support of CAP, 20-21, 32
business deregulation, 139
Butler, Congressman Caldwell, 163

CAA, see Community Action Agency (CAA)
California, gold in, 63
camp, for low-income youth, 102
Campbell, Bob, 160
CAPs, see Community Action Programs
carpentry, OIC job, 73
Carter, President Jimmy, 12, 135, 152
Catholic churches, in Roanoke Valley, 22
caulk, 80
Cave Springs Jaycees, 80
CETA (Comprehensive Employment Training Act), 65, 68-72, 100
CETA funds, for Stop Gap program, 108; for weatherization crews, 80
CETA worker, in Head Start, 94
Chambers, Charlene, 9, 11, 41, 98
Charlotte, NC, 5
child care, 86
child development, and Head Start, 91
child labor, 140
Child Program Board, 97
child support payments, 89
childhood development, in Home Start program, 95
children, behavior of, 91-92; and diseases caused by bad water, 121; employment of, 98; health of, 91, 93; in poverty, 17, 90, 144; recreation for, 61, 102; summer feeding pro-

grams for, 58; see also youth
Children's Home Society School, 87
China, planned economy of, 145
Citizens Anti-Poverty Evaluation Committee, 50-51
City of Roanoke Redevelopment Housing Authority, 81
civil rights movement, 14-15; and local government, 149; and poverty movement, 28
clothing, needed before job creation, 145
clothing programs, of TAP, 52
coal, 23
college entrance, and Project Discovery, 159
Columbia University, 42
community action, 146
Community Action Act, 158
Community Action Agencies (CAAs), 18; and causes of poverty, 28; function of, 19-21; leadership in, 28-43; legacy of, 137-38; versus government agencies, 148-49
community action programs, and poverty, 146-53
Community Action Programs (CAPs), 18, 19; and small business, 32
community control, 18-19
Community Development Block Grant money, 163
Community Diversion Incentive program grant, 158
Community Education, for ex-offenders, 109-10
community gardens program, 74
Community Housing Corporation, 84
community organization, 61-63; training in financing, 124; workers, 62, 63
Community Outreach, 79, 155
community safety, community organizers interest in, 62
community service work, for children, 102
Community Services Administration (CSA), 128, 135
community truck garden program, 58

composting toilets, in Piney River, 127
Comprehensive Employment Training Act, see CETA
Comprehensive Neighborhood Improvement Plan, 80-81
computer keypunching, NYC graduates trained in, 66
computerization, displaces workers, 144
concerts, by Artemis, 88
Congressional Clearinghouse of the Future, 160
consumer education programs, 86, 88
cooperatives, check on capitalism, 141
correctional costs, 148
correctional institutions, in America, 105
cosmetology, NYC graduates trained in, 66
cost, of poverty programs, 148
counseling, for culturally unemployed, 7; for pregnant teenagers, 87; programs under CETA, 69
Covington, pulp mill, 24
craft program, at prison, 111
crafts, for children, 102
Craig County, forestation of, 24
credit workshops, 88
credit union, 59
crime, and poverty link, 147
criminal justice system, and alcoholics, 60
crisis relief, 74
Cruz, Reverend Tom, 155
CSA, see Community Services Administration (CSA)
cultural experiences, for youth, 103
cultural unemployment, 71-72

dance recitals, by Artemis, 88
day care, 9, 34; early TAP plan, 25, see also Head Start
day care centers, for after school care, 25, 95, 96
default prevention, 83
Delaney Court, 156
Delaware, SE/R-CAP member, 128, 157

delinquency prevention grants, 99
Demonstration Water Project (DWP), 122-26, 130
Department of, see under other part of name
Desper, Betty, 76-78, 151, 157
detoxification, 59, 104
diarrhea, caused by bad water, 121
divorce, and poverty, 89
drama, for inmates, 112-14
drinking water, see water
driver's license, for prisoners, 115
Dropout Mobile, 96
dropouts, 65, 100
drug abuse programs, 4, 59-60, 62
drug rehabilitation, and community organizers, 63
drug therapy groups, at Botetourt, 107
DWP, see Demonstration Water Project
dysentery, caused by bad water, 121

Earn and Learn, 98-99
easements, for DWP, 125
East Roanoke, Head Start in, 94
economic conditions, changes in, 144
economic development, STEP, 127
Economic Opportunity Act, 17-18, 19, 32
Edlich, Ted (Theodore J.), 30; appearance of, 6, 9-12; and Atkins, 112; contrast with Hardin, 40-42; as executive director, 159; and Harrison School, 162
education, 34; access to, 17; community organizers interest in, 62; cost effectiveness of, 148; improvements in, needed, 146; minimum needed before job creation, 64, 145; and poverty, 16; of prisoners, 108; part of TAP goal, 52-53; in TAP area, 25; and women, 87-88
Education, U.S. Department of, 159
elderly, 75; poor, 55-56; units for, 85; and weatherization, 80; see also senior citizens
electrical wiring, 81

emergency aid program, of TAP, 74
employment, CAP objective, 20
employment, for ex-offender, 109
employment and training program, of TAP, 133, 159
encounter sessions, 44
encouragement to return to school, of Neighborhood Youth Corps, 65
Energy, U.S. Department of, 80
energy, STEP, 127
energy conservation, counseling on, 82
engineer, role of in DWP, 124
Environmental Protection Agency (EPA), United States, 128
Episcopalian Diocese of Southwest Virginia, 7
Evans Products, 59
eviction prevention, 83
ex-offender, employment for, 109; families of, 106-07; profile of, 114; population of, 75; programs for, 104-119, 160; reentry program for, 107; Stop Gap program, 54; Virginia CARES, see Virginia CARES
eye examination, in Head Start, 93

fair housing ordinance in Roanoke, 85
family planning, 53, 60-61, 71, 86, 87, 127
Family Service-Traveler's Aid, 56
farm families, in poverty, 16; see also rural
Farmer's Home Administration, 77, 82, 84, 122, 123, 125
Fauquier Community Action Agency, 155
Feathers, 112
federal control, over poverty assistance, 149
Federal Housing Administration (FHA), 84-85
Federalist Papers, 150
field trips, for children, 102
Fifth Planning District, 62
film, on Virginia community action agencies, 158
Fincastle, 22, 94

fire prevention program, 73
First Federal Savings and Loan, 163
Fleming High School, 97
Florida, SE/R-CAP member, 128, 157
Floyd County, fuel alcohol plant in, 127
food, minimum needed before job creation, 145
food bill, TAP emergency aid program, 74
food programs, 52, 57-58
food stamp fraud, 139
food stamps, 58, 137, 146
Food-Buying Clubs, CETA staffed, 70
Foodbank, 57-58
food shopping strategy workshops, 88
football, TAP-organized youth program, 102
Ford, President Gerald, 135
Ford, Roger, 11
Ford Foundation, 51, 117, 158
foreclosure, costs of, 84
Forgotten War, The, 159
Forum on Women and Work, 87
foster homes, for adolescents, 97
Franklin County, TAP retreat in, 47; water system in, 125
Friends of VISTA, 160
Friends to Victims of Crime, 108
fuel alcohol plant, 127
fuel assistance, 74, 137
fuel oil spills, handbook on, 128
funding, for community action, 152
Futures Advisory Board, 160

Gainsboro-Northwest Boys and Girls Club, 102
Galbraith, John Kenneth, 140-41
Garland, Senator Ray, 159
G.E.D. (General Equivalency Degree), 70, 88, 100, 111
George, Henry, 141
Georgia, SE/R-CAP member, 128, 157
Gimmeabreak, 112
Gish's Mill, see Vinton
Glasglow, Head Start in, 94
glasses, in Head Start, 93
Global Water, 128

Goldwater, Barry, 132
Goochland, Va., 113
Governor's Employment and Training Council, 115
grade-school children, 96; see also children; and after-school care
Great Society, 16, 132
Greenleigh Associates, report on TAP, 48-50
Grote, George, 4
Guerrant, Herb, 155

Hardin, Bristow, and Desper, 76; heritage of, 164; influence of, 1-12; leadership style of, 35-40; passion for people, 29-30; sensitivity training and, 44-45; and Thomas; 98; and Warren, 129
Hardin, Elizabeth, see Hardin, Teeny
Hardin, John Wesley, 35
Hardin, Teeny, 2-3
Harper, Nancy, 160
Harrington, Michael, 15, 17
Harrison School, 162-64
Harrison School Hazel Thompson History and Cultural Center, 163-64
Harvard University, 42
Head Start, acceptance of today, 133; Charlene Chambers teacher in, 9; curriculum of, 92; Edlich directed, 41; established under Economic Opportunity Act, 18, 71; first program of TAP, 53; goal of social competence, 90; and IQ gains, 95-96; OEO/CSA legacy, 137; parent involvement in, 90, 92; part of war on poverty, 146; records of, 48; and Cleo Stims, 160; work by ex-offenders, 110
Health, Education and Welfare, Department of, 133
health, of children, 91, 93, 121
Health and Human Services (HHS), U.S. Department of, 128, 136
Health Assessment and Prevention Education, CETA staffed, 70
health care, 18, 34; access to, 17; in clinics, 137; in Head Start, 93; in neighborhood centers, 18; in STEP, 127; see also medical care; and Medicaid
health services, community organizers interest in, 62
hearing examination, in Head Start, 93
Hegira House, 4, 105
Heller, Walter, 15
HELP, Inc., 60
Herbert, Dave, 34
Hispanic, OEO administrators, 137
Hodgins, Jere Lee, 112
Hoffman, Bill, 11
Holland, Sara, 155, 159
Hollins College, 156
home improvement programs, 85
home ownership, for poor, 79
home sites, donation of, 84
Home Start program, 95
Homemaker Service Program, 56
homemaker services, 86
homemaking training, 26
Homestead Act, 141
hope, part of TAP philosophy, 53
Hotel Roanoke, 154-55
housing, community organizers interest in, 62; counseling about, 62, 79, 81; improvements needed, 146; problem for poor in Roanoke, 85; rehabilitation, 79, 80-82, 157; rural, 127
Housing and Urban Development (HUD), 81-82, 84, 163
housing code, 62, 79, 81
housing rehabilitation, 79, 80-82, 157
HUD see Housing and Urban Development (HUD)
Human Rights, Department of, 42
Human Services Training, 6
Human Services Training and Technical Assistance, 41
Humphrey, Hubert, 133
hygiene, 44, 102

impetigo, caused by bad water, 121
In School, of Neighborhood Youth Corps, 65

income, of Neighborhood Youth Corps, 65; of women, 85
Indonesia, 160
industrial policy, 153
Industrial Revolution, 140
Industry Bound, 97
initiative, 72
Inmate Job Readiness, Development and Placement Project, 111
Inmate Legal Assistance Program, 111
innoculations, in Head Start, 93
institutionalization of job creation, 64-65
insulation, 80, see also weatherization
insurance, for homes, 84
insurance companies, and pension scales for women, 85
integration efforts, 97, 155
International Drinking Water Supply and Sanitation Decade, 128
Ives, Mike, 76-77

jailers, and TAP, 150
Jefferson, Thomas, 8, 30
Jefferson High School, alternative education at, 100
Jefferson National Forest, 24, 67, 70
Jewish synagogues, in Roanoke Valley, 22
Job Corps, 17, 133
job counseling, early TAP plan, 26
job creation, for poor, 14, 64-65
job preparation, for offenders, 115
Job Research Bank, for ex-offenders, 109
job skills, for ex-offenders, 109
jobs, and economic development, 63-73; and skill match, 144
Johnson, Howard, 10
Johnson, Lyndon B., 13, 133, 141, 142, 143
Johnston, Wally, 122
Jones, Jim, 8
Justice, U.S. Department of, 139
juvenile delinquency, 98

Kennedy, John F., 15

Kimball Renewal Project, 85
kindergarten, 93, 95
King, Martin Luther Jr., 46
Kyle, Joe, 10

labor, support of CAP, 20-21
Labor, U.S. Department of, 65, 68, 133
laboratory aides, trained by New Careers, 68
laboratory technology, NYC graduates trained in, 66
laissez-faire principles, 140
Landstown, Head Start in, 94
Latch Key program, 100-01
laws, and Legal Aid drive to change them, 57
Leach, Ralph, 39
leadership, qualities of successful, 29
League of Older Americans, 157
Legal Aid, 56-57; under OEO, 18; shelter for abused women, 86; Society of the Roanoke Valley, 57
Legal Rights of Women, 87
Legal Services Corporation, 139
Lexington, Head Start in, 94; typical American community, 22
liberals, role for, 153
Lincoln Terrace, Head Start in, 94
local agencies, role of in CAA, 18
local government, 51, 149
loneliness and isolation, of elderly, 56
Lott Carie Foreign Mission Convention, 157
Loudon, Head Start in, 93-94
low-income housing, 79, 81-82

McGuire Stuart Co., 31
Madison, James, 150
Mahala, private corporation, 87
maintenance, by ex-offenders, 110
Marmion, Right Reverend William H., 7-8
Marx, Karl, 143
Maryland, SE/R-CAP member, 128, 157
Mayhew, Gail, 160
Meadows, Georgia, 30, 42-44, 157

means test, for economic assistance, 139
Medicaid, OEO/CSA legacy, 137
medical care, 52, 145, 146; see also health care
medical examination, in Head Start, 93
Medicare, 146
Megatrends, 40
Mental Health Services, 83
mental health services, for alcoholism, 59-60
Mill Mountain Playhouse, 112
minimum wages, 146
ministry, and leadership, 29
minorities, in workforce, 137
money management, for ex-offenders, 109
Montgomery Presbytery, 41
Montvale, Head Start in, 94
moral issue, of poverty, 147
mortgage counseling, 82
mothers' clubs, 86
movies, TAP-organized youth program, 102-03
Mrs. Harrison School, see Thompson, Hazel
Municipal Court of Roanoke, 60
Murray, E. W., 112

NAACP, 48, 155
Nash, Alvin, 155, 159
National Association for the Advancement of Colored People, see NAACP
National Demonstration Water Project (NDWP), 126-27
national forest system, 23
National Institute of Corrections, 158
National Institute for Alcohol and Alcohol Abuse, 59
National Organization for Women, 86
needs assessment process, in DWP, 123
Neighborhood Assistance Act, 158
neighborhood centers, for afterschool care, 25
neighborhood health centers, under OEO, 18
Neighborhood Youth Corps (NYC), 65

neo-liberals, 153
New Careers, for disadvantaged adults, 67-68
New Deal, 14, 17, 64
New Right, 138-40, 143, 152-53
Nickens, Dr. Harry, 156-57
Nixon, Richard, 12, 133, 142, 152
nontraditional jobs, for women, 88-89
Norfolk and Western Railroad, 23, 155
North Carolina, SE/R-CAP member, 128, 157
Northwest Improvement Association, 161
Northwestern University, 42
Norwich Community study, 54
nuclear war, 22
nurses aides, training for, 66, 68
Nutcracker Suite, 103
nutrition, in Head Start, 92-93
nutrition counseling, 58
NYC, see Neighborhood Youth Corps

OEO, see Office of Economic Opportunity
offenders, part of poverty, 144
Office of Community Action, in Va., 158
Office of Economic Opportunity (OEO), alcoholism grant, 59-60; funding for Demonstration Water Project, 122, 126; early funding from, 34; grant, 72; history of, 17-18, 132, 133-34; poor people agency, 122; versus CETA, 69
Ogden, Martha, 155, 159-60
Ogden, Reverend Ely, 156
older workers, 72-73
Olin, Congressman James, 159
Olivarez, Graciela, 135
Operation Homework, 96
Operation Insight, 97
Operation Mainstream, 67
Opportunities Industrialization Center (OIC), 72-73
Opportunities Industrialization Council, 39
organizing, of community action agen-

cies, 160
Ortho-Vent Shoe Company, 31
orthopedic shoes, in Head Start, 93
Our Hope Credit Union, 59
Out of School of Neighborhood Youth Corps, 65
Outreach, CETA program, 69

painting, OIC job, 73
paper hanging, OIC job, 73
parent education, 86
parent involvement, in Head Start, 90, 92
parenting education, for pregnant teenagers, 87
Parents Support Group, 87
Parks Development, CETA staffed, 70
parole supervision, 106
Payne, Osborne, 35, 38-39
peace, 33
Peace Corps, 17
peer aspect, of community action, 151
pension, of women, 85
personality as historical force, 29-30
personnel, in community action, 151
Phillips, Howard, 12, 134-35
Piney River, STEP, 127
Pittsylvania Community Action Agency, 161
planned economy, and poverty, 145
Planned Parenthood, 61
plays, Artemis, 88; see also drama
plumbing, 73, 81, 120-21
poetry readings, by Artemis, 88
police patrols, 79
poor, in CAPs, 20; voiceless, 79
poor families, headed by women, 85
poor neighborhoods, and normal city services, 79
poor people, in Roanoke Valley, 4
poor population, as revolutionary force, 33, 147
poorhouses, 140
Poskocil, Ann, 159
poverty, agenda, for future, 146; attitudes toward, 14-15, 138; and civil rights movement, 14-15, 28; combi-
nation of life conditions, 131; and community action, 146-53; cycle of, 64; and ex-offender, 105-07; indicators, 16-17; national problem, 149; reality of problem, 28; representation in TAP, 47; temporary expedient not working, 143-44; war on, 13-16, 136-39
poverty elimination, and opportunity preserved, 145
pregnancy counseling, 87
pre-vocational training, early TAP plan, 26
prenatal clinic, in Washington County, 127
prison, construction cost of, 148; returning to community, 106; theatre workshops, 113-14
Prison Families Program, 108, 111
prisoner, reeducation and training program cost, 119; returning to community, 106
prisoner rehabilitation, outside the system, 118-19
prisons, 105
Privacy Act of 1974, 82
probation officer, 118
Project Breakthrough, 110
Project Discovery, 159
Project Recovery, for dropouts, 100
promptness, 72
Protestant denominations, in Roanoke Valley, 22
Protestant work ethic, 14
psychological counselors in Head Start, 93
public lands, and Operation Mainstream, 67
Public Service Employment Program, 70, 100
public transportation system, and community organizers, 63
public-private partnerships, 153
pulpwood, in Alleghany County, 24

race, 48, 50, 51
racial discrimination, 17, 140

racial issue, 45-47
racial tension, 63, 97
RADAR, see Roanoke Area Dial-a-Ride
Reading is Fundamental (RIF), 102
Rape Support Group, 87
reading and writing, for adults, 26
reading skills, for children, 102
Reagan, President Ronald, 136, 138, 140-41, 143
Reaganomics, 12
realtors, referral to, 84
recidivism, 105; cause of, 106; cost of, 119, 148; and family, 116; of married ex-offenders, 107; and poverty, 117; rate of, 117; of Stop-Gap participants, 110
recreation programs of TAP, 61-62
referral outreach, 63
rehabilitation of donated housing, 79
reliability, 72
relocation, in emergency, 82
remedial education, for New Careers people, 68
rent bill, TAP emergency aid program, 74
Rent-A-Kid, 100-01
rental payments, counseling on, 82
retail sales, NYC graduates trained in, 66
retarded children, 92
Reynolds, J.C., 122
Richmond Community Action Program, 111
Roanoke, education of, 25; establishment of, 22; etymology of, 23; income of, 24-25; population of, 23
Roanoke & Times World News, 157
Roanoke Area Dial-a-Ride (RADAR), 73
Roanoke City, Department of Parks, 66; jail, 111
Roanoke County Jail, 111
Roanoke NAACP, 155
Roanoke Hotel, 154-55
Roanoke Times, 11, 76
Roanoke Valley, Head Start in, 94;

poverty in, 21-27
Roanoke Valley Council of Community Services, 32, 34, 48, 62
Roanoke Valley Torch Club, 32
Robb, Governor Charles, 158
roofing, OIC job, 73
Roosevelt, President Franklin D., 141, 142
Rubicon drug program, 104-05
rural housing staff, 77-78
rural people, and poor water, 121, 128
rural projects, 127
rural water, 128
Rural Youth Activities, CETA staffed, 70

Sabean, John, 39
Safe Drinking Water Act, 126
Salem, 22; and Brand's reappointment, 51; and Desper, 76; Head Start in, 94
salt deposits, 22
Salvation Army, 58
sanitation, poverty problem, 121
Saunders, Mrs., 6
Saunders, Sherman, 161
Save-a-Buck cooperative, 58
Scholarship Clearinghouse, CETA staffed, 70
Scholastic Aptitude Tests (SAT), 70
school, transition to, 91
school districts, and aliens, 139
school integration, 97
SCOOP, see Senior Citizens Organization for Opportunity Program
SE/R-CAP members, 128, 157
Sears, pickets at, 76
Second Harvest Foodbank Network, 58
secretarial training, 66, 73
segregation, effect of, 63-64
self-worth, NYC graduates trained in, 66
senior citizens, Aid to the Elderly, 101; TAP plans for, 26
Senior Citizens Advisory Council, 155
Senior Citizens Organization for Opportunity Program (SCOOP), 55-56
sensitivity training, 44

sharecropper cooperative, 19
sharecroppers, 63
sheetmetal work, OIC job, 73
shelter, for abused women, 86; minimum needed before job creation, 145; programs of TAP, 52
Shenandoah railway, 28
shopping cart retrieval program, 101
Shriver, Sargent, 17, 19, 32, 132, 160
Sims, Cleo, 160
Sinclair, Upton, 141
skills, for employment, 64
Skinner, B. F., 41
slavery, 140
slaves, as sharecroppers, 63
slums, 140
Small Town Emphasis Project (STEP), 127
Smith, A. Byron, 47
smoke detectors, TAP program on, 73
Social Security, 28, 146
social service programs, 55-61
social services block grant program, and CSA, 136
solar greenhouses, test of, 127
South, poverty in, 16, 28
South Carolina, SE/R-CAP member, 128, 157
Southeast Rural Community Assistance Project (SE/R-CAP), 128, 157
Southeastern Tidewater Opportunity Project, 111
Southwest Virginia Community Development Fund, 57, 72
Southwest Virginia Foodbank, 155, 159
Southwestern State, 104
Soviet Union, peace with, 33; planned economy of, 145
spiritual comfort programs, of TAP, 52
sports, activities for youth, 102
Spouse Abuse, 87
St. John's Episcopal Church, 7, 8, 9, 94
Stamper, Reverend James (Jim), 9, 11
Staunton Correctional Center, 112-13
STEP, 127
Stinson, Elaine, 122
Stop Gap program, 54, 107-110

Storefront, for ex-offenders, 109
storm windows, 80
street crime, 119
street lighting, 79
structural repairs, 81
summer day care, 96
summer feeding programs, for children, 58
Summer Youth Corps, of Neighborhood Youth Corps, 65
Summer Youth Employment Program, 98
surplus cheese program, 58
Swartz, William P., 84
sweatshops, 140
swimming classes, 61
swimming pool construction, 61
swimming pools, 53, 97

Taking Youth Seriously, 100
TAP, 1; see also under other heading; credibility with clients, 45; early plans of, 25-26; evaluation of, 47-51; financial problems of, 51; leadership of, 28-43; local government's contribution to, 51; as program development agency, 53-55; personnel policies of, 46-47; programs of, 52-61; racial equality in, 45-47; staff of, 30-44, 54; tenth anniversary of, 4; style of, 44-45
tap water, 120-31
tax credit, for donations to community action projects, 158
tax laws, and poverty, 139
Taylor, Dr. Noel C., 155
teacher aides, trained by New Careers, 68
technical jobs, 71
teenage lounge, 61
teenagers, and drugs, 59; pregnant, 87
Teeny, see Bristow, Teeny
The Other America, 15
theater, for inmates, 112-14
Thomas, Delegate Vic, 163
Thomas, Jayne, 97-99, 158
Thomas, Anna Mae, 10